WATERLOO TO T
ATLANTIC COAST
DURING THE DIESEL ERA

PART 1

Waterloo to Exeter Central

BERNARD MILLS

Published by Platform 5 Publishing Ltd,
52 Broadfield Road, Sheffield, S8 0XJ. England.
Printed in England by The Amadeus Press, Cleckheaton, West Yorkshire.
ISBN: 978 1 915984 14 2

Front cover top: Only a few weeks before the Class 42 Warships finished operating on services between London Waterloo and Exeter St Davids, on 25 August 1971, D811 "Daring" races round the curve beneath Battledown Flyover with 1O10, the 10.10 Exeter–Waterloo. This photogenic location, which is to the west of Basingstoke, is examined in more detail in Chapter 1.

Front cover bottom: On the morning of 29 March 1975, D1036 "Western Emperor" points east and towards the newly-modified track layout at the Up end of Yeovil Junction. The train is standing at the station's former Up bay platform which had been converted to a new through platform just three days earlier. Class 52 "Westerns" were not a regular fixture on the former London & South Western Railway's route between Waterloo and Exeter and D1036 was visiting with the "Western Sunset" railtour, which had arrived from Plymouth and was about to veer north towards Yeovil Pen Mill and beyond.

Back cover: Like their diesel-hydraulic predecessors, the diesel-electric Class 50s have very much been part of the story of the Waterloo to Exeter line. With its original number D400 visible on the near cab side, 50050 approaches the former Seaton Junction station with 1O41, the 16.22 Exeter–Waterloo on 27 July 1991. The locomotive had been taken out service the previous summer and appeared to have worked its last train, but in the light of the popularity of the class and 50050 being the first example to be built, its repairs were sanctioned. At the same time it was repainted into this livery, which replicates how it looked when it was completed in 1967 after a successful campaign to raise the funds needed for the repaint. It had returned to service wearing this new look three months earlier, in April 1991. More details and photographs of this location can be found in Chapter 3.

Above: A successful visit to Battledown on 25 August 1971 produced the bonus of a Hymek, when D7030 was captured racing past with 1O26, the 09.30 Birmingham New Street–Poole. The engine would work through to Poole and return with its Western Region crew on a corresponding northbound working. In 1971 time was running out for the Hymeks, as it was for the Warships, on these forays into Southern Region territory. It was a heyday that was cut short.

Right: Plenty of locations along the route that we are exploring have seen little change in recent decades, but mother nature provides plenty of variety through her never-ending seasonal cycle. Spring has begun in the rolling Wiltshire countryside as 33109 pulls a 4TC set away from Tisbury with 1L07, the 12.10 Waterloo–Gillingham on 15 April 1989. This formation of train will be explained when we reach Gillingham in Chapter 2.

Title page: In the final full year of locomotive hauled trains on the route from Waterloo to Exeter, this scene in the charming valley of the River Nadder is representative of the short-lived but very colourful Network SouthEast era. Passing through Tisbury Gates on 10 June 1992 is 47711 with 1O34, the 08.11 Exeter St Davids–Waterloo on 10 June 1992.

■CONTENTS

Chapter 1

A look at the first 51¾ miles of the journey to the West of England, to the point where the Bournemouth line deviates. On this busy section, diesels share the tracks with the third rail electric trains that travel through the leafy suburbs of commuter land.

Chapter 2

The journey west continues through a more rural landscape and includes a focus on Salisbury, before traversing the predominantly single track main line to Yeovil.

Chapter 3

The route forward from Yeovil travels into England's more westerly counties. Various forms of diesel motive power are illustrated along this part of the route which has changed greatly during the timescale covered by this book.

◼ INTRODUCTION

Welcome to volume one of "Waterloo to the Atlantic Coast in the Diesel Era". In this book we shall examine the route from London Waterloo to Exeter Central via Salisbury, seeing a variety of motive power through the era that began with the diesel hydraulic classes and continues to today's Class 159 Sprinters. The vast majority of the content will however be of locomotive-hauled trains. In the second volume, unlike the steam companion to this two-part series (published by Platform 5 in 2022), we shall not change at Exeter St Davids to head west on the former Great Western Railway (GWR) main line, but will continue on ex-London & South Western Railway (L&SWR) and Southern Railway (SR) metals to reach the extremities of the Atlantic Coast, known more colloquially as "The Withered Arm".

Colour photography for me began in May 1965, when 10 months into what would become a 57-year railway career, I had saved enough money from my position as a junior clerk in the Parcels Office at Plymouth to purchase a decent camera. This was a Praktica IV Single Lens camera with a Domiplan lens, which at £46 (£750 using 2024 prices) was a severe dent in the finances of a young worker in the mid-1960s! It was however, worth every penny and despite its now cumbersome appearance and the clanking of its mirrors, it was state of the art in 1965 and one of the first SLRs to be seen amongst the local railway photographers of the time. I remember showing it off at a Railway Correspondence & Travel Society (RCTS) meeting in Exeter, where my great friend and celebrated photographer the late Peter Gray, gave it a close examination. Four years later I upgraded to the latest Praktica model which came with a superior Tessar lens. This did me well for the next 18 years until the Olympus OM1 came on the scene with its even higher quality. The latter was only retired in 2010 when I made the move to digital photography with a Canon EOS 5D.

To produce a journey from London Waterloo to the remotest parts of the station's former empire has proved to be a challenge. Obviously not all locations along the route can be depicted or described, so I have had to make some hard choices on what to insert and what to bypass. Room has been made for locations that aren't so well known, along with some rare colour images of particular motive power or photos that have a story to tell, which I hope adds to readers' enjoyment. Each of the pictures in this book are of my own taking. I should add that the quality of images that we have become accustomed to in the age of digital photography, especially in unfavourable weather conditions, was unachievable in the 1960s. Back in the days of film, one was limited by the ISA rating of the film that was available. Fortunately, the tools now available to scan and improve these precious pictures have not only helped to preserve my colour slides, but they either enhance them or in some cases, simply provide an acceptable result. Those who created digital cameras and editing software should in my opinion be called saints! A handful of images that aren't quite up to the mark have been included where they depict something that is either particularly historic or impossible to replicate today. I hope that you enjoy the golden oldies!

For those not familiar with railway operating terms and the four character headcode system that is regularly referred to in this book, I would like to add a few basic notes. An Up train is one travelling in the direction of London, although the capital may not be its final destination. Similarly, a Down train is one travelling away from London, but it may not have originated there. Take the Halwill to Bude branch as an example. A train making the journey from Halwill to Bude is a Down train, because it is heading away from London. Likewise, a Bude to Halwill service is an Up train, because even though its destination is within Devon, it is travelling in the direction towards London. The system that uses four character headcodes to identify individual trains was Introduced in June 1960 and remains in use on the national network today. The first character is a number denoting the class of the train; Class 1 trains are express passenger or newspaper services, Class 2 are stopping passenger services, Class 3 carry parcels, fish or fruit etc. or are empty coaching stock with train crew, Class 4 are express freights, Class 5 are empty coaching stock and Classes 6 to 9 are for various types of freight or special loads. If the first digit is a zero, that indicates a light engine movement. The second character is a letter that denotes the train's destination area, unless it is a Z which indicates a special non-timetabled working such as a railtour. The third and fourth characters of the headcode are two numbers which complete the train's individual code. Train headcodes don't give any indication as to whether it is for an Up or Down service.

I must thank those who have assisted in the research, preparation and creation of this book. I am particularly grateful to Jeremy Clark for his help with the software, and to Roger Geach and Barry Jones for their assistance in scanning and editing the images. My thanks also go to John Fissler for his help with matters of signalling and research, and for his time given over to proof reading; to Martin Street for train and headcode identification, and his encyclopaedic knowledge of the Class 42 and 43 diesels, to Tony Wardle for his knowledge and research freely imparted, to Graham Bowden for sharing his valued knowledge of signalling around Crediton, to Colin Marsden for his help with SR matters and electric trains in particular, to Richard Green and his friends around Basingstoke, David Tozer from Crewkerne and Richard Burningham of the Devon & Cornwall Railway Partnership. My thanks also go to Andy Chard and his colleagues at Platform 5 for their help, guidance and this high quality finished article. If I have overlooked anyone who has contributed in any way with information and/or advice, please accept my apologies. Much information has come from my own notebooks and useful reference sources such as the timetables of the day.

Bernard Mills
Devon, Early 2024

Above: A scene typical of the 1980s, at the advent of the Network SouthEast era; 50020 "Revenge" hurries along one of the few remaining double track sections between Salisbury and Exeter on 4 October 1986. It is bringing 1O19, the 09.38 Exeter St Davids–Waterloo down from the summit at Milborne Port to Templecombe, where the restrictive single track line will restart. The train includes a sign of things to come, as its penultimate coach has recently gained the new Network SouthEast livery. The formation comprises decent motive power and comfortable rolling stock with windows that one could open, allowing enthusiasts to enjoy the music from the head of the train, something that has now become taboo. Within six years Revenge would be no more, being scrapped at C F Booth of Rotherham in June 1992. A year and a month later, Class 159 Sprinters would take over from loco-hauled trains on the route.

■ ABBREVIATIONS

Abbreviations

ASC – Area Signalling Centre
B&W – Bodmin & Wadebridge Railway
BR – British Railways/British Rail
DMU – Diesel Multiple Unit
DEMU – Diesel Electric Multiple Unit
EMU – Electric Multiple Unit
GWR – Great Western Railway
HST – High Speed Train
L&SR – London & Southampton Railway
L&SWR – London & South Western Railway

M&SWJR – Midland & South Western Junction Railway
NSE – Network South East
PSB – Panel Signal Box
PRC – Plymouth Railway Circle
RCTS – Railway Correspondence & Travel Society
ROC – Rail Operations Centre
SR – Southern Railway
TOPS – Total Operating Processing System
WR – Western Region

CHAPTER 1 -
THE SOUTH WESTERN MAIN LINE: FROM WATERLOO TO BATTLEDOWN FLYOVER

Much has been written about the grand L&SWR London Terminus of Waterloo elsewhere, with plenty in the corresponding steam volume, so there is little need to repeat this here. Situated in the London Borough of Lambeth, Waterloo opened on 11 July 1848, on the extension of the line from the previous terminus at Nine Elms. The L&SWR designed the station with the intention that its route would be extended further into London, but the authorities would have none of it. The L&SWR did eventually get into the commercial heart of the capital by way of the short underground Waterloo & City Railway, which ran from a separate lower-level terminus to Bank. This had opened on 8 August 1898 and the L&SWR took it over on New Year's Day 1907. The line was later transferred to the ownership of British Rail (BR) and then to London Underground Ltd on 1 April 1994, and it remains in operation today. As traffic levels grew over the years, Waterloo station was extended. To cut the story of this short, work

commenced in 1903 and the rebuilt spacious terminus that we know today was formally opened by Queen Mary, wife of George V, on 21 March 1922. The station would see further changes during the 1990s as detailed later in this chapter.

As the title of this book implies, this is where our journey to the Atlantic Coast during the diesel era begins. The Southern Railway (SR) was an early pioneer of diesel power. Its last Chief Mechanical Engineer, O. V. Bulleid, had an eye on the future with this, when in February 1947 he obtained authority to construct two main line diesel locomotives. These emerged from Ashford Works three years later, by which time the SR was now the Southern Region of BR. Numbered 10201 and 10202, these were known as the Class D16/2 and saw limited use on expresses from Waterloo to both Bournemouth and Exeter Central, becoming the first diesel hauled trains from London to the West Country. Joined by a third loco 10203 in 1954, the trio were then despatched to the London

Above: The railway in transition. Steam and diesel ran alongside each other out of Waterloo for the better part of three years. During August 1966, Merchant Navy Class 4-6-2 35026 "Lamport & Holt Line" waits with a service to Bournemouth, while Class 42 D867 "Zenith" backs on to the stock for the 13.08 to Exeter St Davids. It is surprising just how short the lives of both engines were, 35026 emerged in its rebuilt form in January 1957, while D867 entered traffic only four years later on 26 April 1961. 35026 would be withdrawn after only a decade in service in its rebuilt guise and the new-fangled diesels would be here forever would they not? In fact D867 only lasted until 18 October 1971, again after just a decade in service. Note behind 35026 the once-familiar landmark of Waterloo signal box. The impressive box opened on 18 October 1936, with 309 levers that were split across three frames. The frames were taken out of use on 5 February 1984 and were replaced by a temporary panel. The box later closed on 30 October 1990, so it could be demolished as part of the International Station build. Control of the area's signalling then passed to the Wimbledon Signalling Centre on 21 April 1991.

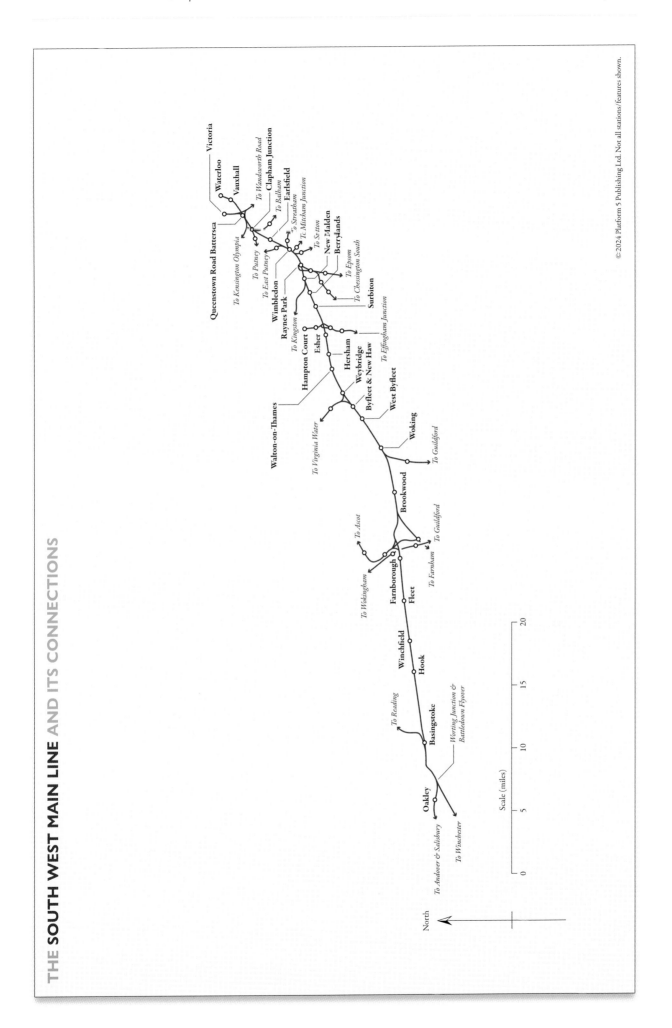

THE SOUTH WEST MAIN LINE AND ITS CONNECTIONS

Midland Region's Camden Shed (1B) in 1955. They remained in service until 1963, when they were withdrawn due to being non-standard. They did leave a legacy however, as 10203 was a template for what became the BR Class 40.

Two years after 10201 and its Class D16/2 colleagues had moved on, the first displacement of steam locomotives took place on the Southern Region's lines to the West Country. This wasn't a major event that affected passenger trains and was far from the hustle and bustle of the capital. On 7 September 1957, Plymouth Friary shed (72D and later 83H) received its first Class 04 diesel shunter, number 11225. This was the first replacement for the depot's aging B4 Class shunting tank engines. There was logic to this deployment; the main duties of the B4 tanks had been working the line from Plymouth Friary to Cattewater, which only ever carried freight. This served a heavily industrialised area that included oil refineries and tar works, bringing a much higher fire risk. The B4s had therefore been fitted with spark arrestors, but this early use of diesel motive power was a much more effective method of reducing the risk of fire. It was a small

and not well-known step for the Southern Region, but it was the first use of diesel motive power in the West Country nonetheless. It wasn't until the following year that the Western Region saw its first diesel motive power in the West Country; that came with much hype and few realised that the Southern Region had already beaten its counterpart to it, albeit on a small scale to serve the needs of industry. I should add that the same month, September 1957, saw the first diesel-worked daily passenger services to be seen at some stations on the route, namely the Class 205 (3H) Hampshire Units that worked local Andover–Southampton and Portsmouth–Salisbury services, although these had little effect on the West of England route at the time.

The transition from steam to diesel did not happen overnight and two events in particular steered the changes on the route from Waterloo to the West Country. From 1 January 1963, all former SR lines west of Wilton South (the first station west of Salisbury) were transferred to BR's Western Region, effectively cutting the Waterloo to Exeter main line into two. The second was the publication of the infamous Beeching Report in March 1963,

Below: This photograph shows the three different forms of traction that Waterloo saw during the 1960s. It was taken on the same day as the previous image and was the only occasion that I captured steam, diesel and electric trains together at any location. D867 waits with the 13.08 to Exeter St Davids, West Country Class 4-6-2 34102 "Lapford" is ready to take the empty stock from a Bournemouth train to Clapham Junction and beyond these is a Southern Railway 4-SUB EMU. The latter is likely to be set 4660, as it is fitted with a roller blind route indicator; only three of the units were so fitted and the other two were working on the Central Section of the Southern Region at the time. The unit is arriving on the Windsor Lines side of the station with a service from Kingston or Hounslow.

Above: With just over a week before the Warships ended their tenure on the West of England expresses, we find a calm and placid scene at Waterloo on 24 September 1971. The morning rush hour has come and gone, as D819 "Goliath" rests at the stop blocks after working 1O08, the 07.20 from Exeter St Davids (which from hereafter will be referred to simply as Exeter in train working details). The loco will be released once the stock has left as the 13.08 departure, before it will be attached to the coaches that form the 15.08 to Exeter. I often wonder what the former Southern Railway men thought of engines built at the Great Western Railway's (GWR) Swindon Works, with their former rival's western pedigree plying its way in and out of Waterloo, as it did at London Paddington. Whoever would have thought, even if it was only for a brief period of seven years, that identical traction would work from both termini? Even though L&SWR/SR and GWR relations thawed over time, they never reached that level of co-operation. BR's Southern Region did however, import several ex-GWR 57xx 0-6-0 Pannier Tanks (a maximum of 15, but not all at the same time), between February 1959 and August 1963. These were allocated to Nine Elms shed (70A) for shunting and empty stock workings to and from Clapham Junction, which brought them into Waterloo. Thus the Class 42 Warships were not the first Swindon design to be seen there. The class also appeared in fits and starts at a third London Terminal, Marylebone, but that is another story.

followed by its implementation and the resulting line and station closures. The route from Waterloo to the Withered Arm, especially that west of Salisbury, would see significant change during the 1960s. It began the decade as a two-track main line and a bastion of steam, and would end the decade as a diesel route, after much of it had been heavily cut back.

Vauxhall is the first station after Waterloo, being 1.75 miles from the terminus, in a spacious setting amid many high-rise office blocks. It has eight tracks, each of which serve a platform and has long been a popular venue for railway photographers. Situated in the borough of Lambeth, it was opened on 11 July 1848 as part of the extension from Nine Elms to Waterloo. It was named Vauxhall Bridge, due to it being adjacent to the bridge of that name over the River Thames. The station suffered severe fire damage on 13 April

1856, but was rebuilt remarkably quickly, then in 1862 the Bridge suffix was dropped from its name. During the second half of 1890, the L&SWR's half-yearly report reported that the widening of the railway between Waterloo and Nine Elms had been completed. This included the enlargement and rearrangement of Vauxhall station over the preceding six years and had cost £600,000, a very substantial sum in 1890. Today's layout came about with the further remodelling that took place in 1936, when the lines to and from Waterloo were realigned and resignalled. Today Vauxhall is served by a high frequency of local services and long-distance trains do not call there due to its proximity to Waterloo. It is a transport hub in its own right, after becoming an interchange with the London Underground on 23 July 1971, when the Victoria Line opened below ground level and there is a busy bus station at street level.

Above: This is Waterloo in transition, as seen from the roof of Canterbury House, which is visible behind the 4-SUB EMU in the above 1966 photograph. 47307 is leaving with the 16.35 to Yeovil Junction on 21 July 1992. It is just as well it's a warm sunny day, as 47/3s have no train heating equipment. The sub-class normally earned their living on freight duties, such as hauling coal to power stations. 47307 was therefore a very rare visitor to Waterloo. At the time, there was something that could be best described as a locomotive crisis, with "all hands to the pump" on workings from Waterloo to Salisbury and beyond, when the transition to Class 159 DMUs was nigh. A line up of EMUs of the period can be seen in the station, waiting to take the commuters home. Waterloo was chosen as the Eurostar terminus ahead of the opening of the Channel Tunnel. This involved substantial construction work at the station, with a brand new five-platform terminal taking over the former Windsor Lines side. Its platforms were numbered 20 to 24, continuing the numerical sequence, but it was branded separately as Waterloo International and came under the management of London & Continental Railways. The station was ready by May 1993, but delays to the completion of the Channel Tunnel meant that it did not open until 14 November 1994, when Eurostar services began. Even though a huge amount was spent on the new terminal, it was only used for 13 years. It closed on 13 November 2007 when the High Speed 1 route was completed and Eurostar services were transferred to London St Pancras. Ownership of Waterloo International passed to Network Rail, which at the time saw no future for it. Over Christmas 2013 the former Eurostar platforms were used, while the main station underwent substantial engineering work. Due to increased passenger numbers, the five former Eurostar platforms were then returned to regular use between 2014 and 2019.

Above right: On 21 March 1991, 33114 displays the Southern Region 62 headcode, which indicates a service on the Waterloo to Salisbury and Exeter route. It is in fine fettle, passing through Vauxhall on the Down Main line with the 16.15 Waterloo–Yeovil Junction. On the far left one can spot Big Ben alongside the Houses of Parliament. The cynical side of me says that more hot air would come out of there than the hard working diesel!

Right: On the same day and at the same place, but looking in the other direction, 50017 "Royal Oak" rumbles past with an empty stock working from Clapham Junction which will form a rush hour service from Waterloo. Standing on its elevated platforms, one gains little impression that the station is actually built on the Waterloo to Nine Elms Viaduct. The railway was constructed in this manner to lessen its impact on the number of the properties that existed here, although there was still a need for the clearance of about 700 of these to enable the L&SWR to reach its London terminal.

Opposite page: These two pictures were taken from a convenient car park on Deeley Road, at the west end of New Covent Garden Market, with London's skyline forming an impressive backdrop. The market was established in November 1974 on the site of the former Nine Elms steam shed (70A) and the L&SWR's original Nine Elms terminus. Needless to say, there is now no evidence of either, such was the transformation of the area. Firstly we see 50027 "Lion" heading west with 1V11, the 11.00 Waterloo–Exeter on 21 March 1991, just four months before the loco was withdrawn. The Eurostar was surely the longest and most exotic train to run on this part of the former-L&SWR main line, albeit only on the first couple of miles of the route. Behind the photographer, the international trains would take a brand new connection to meet the route between London Victoria and the Kent Coast. 3222 & 3221 are seen on an unidentified working on 4 May 1995. Note that in the four years between the two pictures there have been changes to the scene, including the removal of the two lineside huts opposite 50027 and its train. This impressive sight was relatively short-lived, only lasting 12 years to November 2007, when London St Pancras became the new Eurostar terminal. I find it remarkable that such a modern scene is already history.

Above: This was the view from the same car park on Deeley Road, looking west on 21 March 1991, as 50017 "Royal Oak" passes with 1O35, the 09.45 Exeter–Waterloo. The construction work that is taking place to the right of the train was for the new ramp that would take Eurostar services onto the Kent Coast line. Behind the rear of the train the first of the two bridges that carry the metals from London Victoria over the L&SWR main line can be picked out and just beyond that is Queenstown Road Battersea station, our next port of call

Above: A location that is rarely captured on film is the next station after Vauxhall, namely Queenstown Road in the borough of Battersea, which is just over 2.5 miles from Waterloo. Opened 1 November 1877, it is very much an inner suburban station that is served by only two platforms, although there are plans to bring a third back into use to reduce congestion on the two slow lines. It is a dull late morning as 50049 "Defiance" completes the final stage of its journey with the 08.11 from Exeter. The date is 30 July 1991, which is near the end of the era when Class 50s were the motive power on West of England services. The train is passing beneath the substantial bridge that carries the lines out of London Victoria. This is a complex area of railway lines, with those from two London termini continuing the short distance to the next station in the Borough of Battersea, which is much busier and rather more famous.

Below left: So to Clapham Junction, which is just under four miles from Waterloo, with its claim of being the busiest station in the world in terms of the number of trains passing through. It is formed of two separate railways, the south western side is controlled by Wimbledon Area Signalling Centre (ASC) and the south central lines are controlled from Victoria ASC. Furthermore, it is not actually in Clapham, but within the Borough of Battersea. The most convenient way to reach Clapham, which is about a mile away, is to join the metaphorical "man on the Clapham Omnibus". Clapham residents often find the direct train services from Clapham High Street into Victoria more convenient for reaching the capital. In the final fortnight of the Class 42 Warship era on the West of England route, D819 "Goliath" heads west though Clapham Junction with 1V17, the 17.00 Waterloo–Exeter on 23 September 1971. Note the small yellow destination board on the side of the first coach which bears the legend "Waterloo–Salisbury–Exeter". The line through here was built by the London & Southampton Railway (L&SR) as part of its new line from Nine Elms to Woking. When this opened on 21 May 1838, the L&SR became the L&SWR. The first actual junction here was that of the line to Richmond, which opened 27 July 1846 and a station was not deemed to be necessary due to it being a rural location. A major expansion of the site took place with the opening of the London Brighton & South Coast Railway's (LB&SCR) new route out of the capital on 1 October 1860, this running parallel to the L&SWR main line at this point. The extension of the West London Railway over the Thames brought about the construction of the station and Clapham Junction opened with the West London Railway on 2 March 1863. The station was a joint venture between the L&SWR, the LB&SCR and the GWR. The aim was to attract custom from the growth of fashionable housing in these parts and also to afford better interchange of freight traffic off the West London line. Bearing in mind that the L&SWR had a history of spite and enmity with both the LB&SCR and the GWR, this would have been quite an achievement at the time and required a thawing of relations all around. This view looks towards Waterloo and shows the maze of tracks at this point. A notable landmark is Clapham Junction A Signal Box on the left, which straddled some of the tracks. This gave grave cause for concern on 10 May 1965, when it partially collapsed and temporary supporting trestles had to be installed. It survived until all the former L&SWR lines in the area were placed under the control of the Wimbledon ASC over the Bank Holiday weekend of 26–27 May 1990.

Above: This may not be one of my better pictures, but it has been included as this was the only time I ever saw a Class 25 at Clapham Junction. Allocated to the London Midland Region's D01 London Division at the time, D7626 is coming off the West London line with a train primarily formed of BR vans on 23 September 1971. Advice from Colin Marsden suggests that 6O07 could be an incorrect headcode, because at the time 6O07 was a cement train that arrived on Southern Region metals at New Kew Junction. This is almost certainly the Rugby vans, which would be split at Clapham Junction Yard, with some vans going forward to Southampton and the rest to Kent. It was one of the few turns that Willesden-based train crews worked to Clapham Yard. Inter-regional van trains were usually left at Kensington Olympia for the Southern Region to take forward. As there were no Southern Region-based crews trained on Class 25s, D7626 would have headed for home rather than any further into the Southern Region. Many people may not be aware that there was another Clapham Junction hidden away in the West Riding of Yorkshire, where the Little North Western Railway, as it is known, from Carnforth to Skipton via Wennington, met the line from Ingleton. This ceased to be a junction for passengers on 1 February 1954 and for goods in July 1966, when the Ingleton to Low Gill route closed completely. The station remains open today for passengers; the junction suffix has been dropped but it is still referred to locally as Clapham Junction. The peace of the Pennine foothills contrasts sharply with the suburbia of this Clapham. If one were to spend an hour at the southern Clapham Junction during the evening rush hour about 200 trains would pass. To see that many at its northern namesake would require nearly two weeks!

Left: Clapham Junction may claim to be the busiest station in the world, based on the sheer number of trains that pass through each day, but there was nothing of the hustle and bustle during the lunchtime calm on 21 March 1991. 50017 "Royal Oak" provides the only movement with an empty stock working from Waterloo behind the blissfully unaware handful of passengers who are waiting for their respective trains. Note the décor and station furniture of the Network SouthEast era, all of which are now part of the station's history.

Below left: The lunchtime calm extended to the vast array of stock sidings in the yard on the Up side of the South Western lines. One could obtain a good view of proceedings from the station's substantial and still extant footbridge. This was a good time of day to be at Clapham Junction, as plenty of stock would be lined up ready to emerge for the evening rush hour workings. On 30 July 1991, the display of motive power and multiple units was very different from that of today; from left to right are 47709, 50050, a Class 442 Wessex Electric EMU and 2HAP units 4322 & 4314.

Above: Berrylands station is 11 miles from Waterloo and a comparative newcomer on the scene, opening in the era of the Southern Railway on 16 October 1933. It was built to serve the ever expanding housing developments in this part of Kingston upon Thames and Surbiton East could have been an alternative name. On the Down Main line 50031 "Hood" thunders past the wooden platforms with 1V13, the 13.15 Waterloo–Exeter on 12 July 1991, at a time when the class was becoming rarer by the day on these duties. 50031 would be withdrawn from BR service the following week, but fortunately the loco survives in preservation. With its platforms on the slow lines, Berrylands is only served by local services, most of which are Waterloo to Hampton Court trains. To travel west from here, passengers therefore have to change at Surbiton and Woking for West of England services.

Above: The line from Clapham Junction to Basingstoke had been quadrupled by July 1905, with the fast lines being the middle pair and the Up and Down Slow lines being on either side. A mile on from Berrylands in leafy Surrey, D819 "Goliath" is seen from King Charles Road bridge as it approaches Surbiton with 1V13, the 13.00 Waterloo–Exeter on 16 August 1969. The original station was named Kingston and opened on 21 May 1838. It was to the east, being moved to its present site about a quarter of a mile away seven years later. Surbiton is within the borough of Kingston-Upon-Thames, the corporation of which opposed the arrival of the L&SWR, lest it would harm the coaching trade. This forced the railway to pass about a mile and a half south of the town. Like many other localities that objected to the railway piercing their territory, this was soon found to be a mistake, because once the railway opened, the coaching trade collapsed almost overnight. After various renamings the station became Surbiton after Kingston got its own station on the branch from Twickenham in 1867. At the time, the area was rural and the station served a farm and little else, however the trend for people to move from the capital to the greener suburbs was already underway and traffic levels grew.

Above right: The view of a train entering Surbiton station from the east has always been characterised by the fine Ewell Road Bridge. This elegant structure, which is visible in the background and almost forms a small viaduct, is a companion to the similar King Charles Road bridge. The latter is just out of sight and the location from which the previous photograph of D819 was taken. The leafy background blends well with the colours of the Network SouthEast era, as 50017 speeds through with 1V11, the 11.00 Waterloo–Exeter on 12 July 1991.

Right: On the same day as the previous photograph, we turn around to see the now very suburban Surbiton station, which is 12 miles from Waterloo. Today's layout is the result of a 1937 rebuild by the SR, as part of the improvements made when the main line to Woking was electrified. Surbiton station is a superb example of 1930s Art Deco architecture and holds Grade II listed status. A Class 50 that had a special following amongst the enthusiasts of the day, and one that sadly did not escape the cutter's torch, is 50046 "Ajax". The loco passes Surbiton with the 08.11 Exeter–Waterloo on 12 July 1991. The mix of the engine's Large Logo livery and the Network SouthEast coaches brighten the scene during a dull interlude of weather. Although the station is now surrounded by more modern buildings, its Art Deco features are still evident, as the splendid footbridge illustrates. Most long distance trains do not call here, but the station is served by a variety of local and limited semi-fast services, and it is very well used.

Above: Staying in the Surrey commuter belt, we move five miles down the line to another location not often caught on camera to see D826 "Jupiter" passing through Weybridge at speed with 1V15, the 15.08 Waterloo–Exeter on 22 September 1971. The station lies 19¼ miles from Waterloo and is only served by platforms on the Up and Down Slow lines. Situated in the borough of Elmbridge, it opened along with the London & Southampton Railway (L&SR) on 21 May 1838. Weybridge became a junction upon the opening of the Chertsey Branch on 14 February 1848 (this was later extended to Virginia Water), the beginning of which is visible on the left. The line via Chertsey and Virginia Water provides an alternative route to Waterloo via Staines and connections for Reading. Access to this line from the west is achieved by a spur to the east of the next station, Byfleet & New Haw, although this is only used by freight services and when passenger trains are diverted during engineering works. Trains on the West of England Line use this route on a semi-regular basis as the situation demands. Weybridge remains a busy commuter station today, with a choice of services and routes to Waterloo. I am pleased to report that this view has hardly changed and this location is one of the few where expanding vegetation has not left its mark. The motive power may not be so interesting though. This is a good time to mention the third rail electrification, as the L&SWR was an early pioneer in this field. Due to increasing suburban passenger demand, the first route to be so treated was that from Waterloo to East Putney in 1915. As far as our journey to the West Country is concerned, the section between Clapham Junction and Wimbledon (and Strawberry Hill) followed on 30 January 1916, then on 18 June of that year the third rail reached Hampton Court Junction. It was under the Southern Railway that electrification was extended to Woking (and Guildford & Farnham) on 3 January 1937, which meant that Pirbright Junction, to the west of Brookwood, was as far as trains on the West of England Line ran beside the third rail. The limit was then extended 30 years later when BR electrified the line to Bournemouth in July 1967. From then, West of England trains shared the third rail route as far as Worting Junction, to the west of Basingstoke, where Bournemouth services deviate.

Below: The sign says "Network SouthEast Welcome to Woking". The modern developments of this ever expanding town bear no relation to the locality that gave the station its original name. When it opened as the then limit of the L&SR from Nine Elms on 21 May 1838, it was called Woking Common, reflecting the rural nature of the community at the time. The station, which is 24.5 miles from Waterloo, initially only had a single platform and was surrounded by open heath, lying over a mile from the village known as Old Woking. It became a through station when the L&SR was extended to a new railhead at Shapley Heath (now Winchfield) on 24 September 1838, and a junction on 5 May 1845, by which time the Common suffix had been dropped when the line to Guildford was opened. Incidentally, the London & Southampton Railway was renamed the London & South Western Railway because it had its eye on spreading its sphere of operation to the Portsmouth area. Portsmouth's fathers and the Admiralty were horrified at the prospect of a railway to the town which bore the name of its rival port Southampton, so the name was changed to appease the objectors and give a better indication of the company's ambitions. The railway brought prosperity to Woking and the station grew in importance over time as a railhead for the surrounding area. The BR Summer timetable for 1953, which could almost be a repeat of the Southern Railway's timetable, contains a note indicating that Woking is the station for Chobham (3.25 miles away) and Woking Village (1.5 miles). It certainly serves a greater population today. Woking has always been a flat junction, a situation causing at times congestion and delays especially after the line through it was quadrupled. Like Surbiton, the SR completely rebuilt Working station between 1936 and 1937, giving it the Art Deco "Odeon" style that it retains today. All trains to and from the West of England now call here, which was not the case in the steam era; this only changed with the dieselisation of the route in September 1964. My picture depicts 50002 "Superb", with a fine rake of Mark 2a coaching stock slowing for the station call with the 08.40 Waterloo–Exeter on 12 July 1991. Happily the engine remains in preservation on the South Devon Railway and is at present undergoing overhaul.

Above: Here we have more variety at Woking and a throwback to the days before Class 66s, mobile phones and the internet. In Railfreight Distribution livery, 47297 puts on a fine display of exhaust as it powers past with a lengthy Freightliner working that is travelling towards London on 12 July 1991. It would have come from the Southampton area, sharing the tracks from Worting Junction with trains from Salisbury and Exeter. To the right, stabled in the yard are 73108 and 33002, both of which are in grey and yellow Dutch Departmental livery.

Below left: A swift passage of 23.5 miles from Woking brings us to Basingstoke, on the outskirts of which we have a dose of pure nostalgia back in the diesel hydraulic era. On 25 August 1971, D811 "Daring" approaches Basingstoke with 1V17, the 17.00 Waterloo–Exeter, at the point where the Eastern Ring Road now crosses the railway. This view is sadly no longer available due to vegetation and tree growth. Pausing to reflect on the Warship era on the former L&SWR metals, the Swindon-built Class 42 Warships (D800–D832 & D866–D870) were diagrammed for the Waterloo to Exeter workings, with the exception of D800, 801 and 802 due to their lower rated engine power. The North British-built Class 43 version (D833 to D865) made the occasional rare appearance, but they were not banned from the route as has been implied in some quarters. Class 43 workings on the line would have been limited though, because as far as I know, Waterloo-based crews were not trained on them and thus would not have signed Class 43s. In contrast, as far as Warships were concerned, the Paddington to Worcester & Hereford workings were very much the domain of the Class 43s, with only one confirmed Class 42 working having taken place on the Cotswolds route – and that took two locomotive failures before it happened!

Above: Moving few hundred yards closer to the station we find D818 "Glory" in charge of 1V15, the 15.08 Waterloo–Exeter, also on 25 August 1971. This loco is the one that nearly got away, surviving the mass cull and cutting up of the class in the early 1970s by becoming, for want of a better word, the Swindon Works' pet. It was looked after by a group of employees who repainted it into green livery and hoped to preserve it. After outliving most of its classmates by more than a decade, it finally met its fate at Swindon in 1985. On the left are the still extant Barton Mill Carriage Sidings. Parked up and awaiting the call to reinforce the afternoon rush hour services is a Class 423 4-VEP EMU. These were first introduced in 1967 for the newly-electrified line to Bournemouth and are best described as a slam-door Mark 1 coach electric unit. They survived into the 21st century, working their last service on 26 May 2005. Whether their present day replacements are any better or as comfortable is a moot point.

Above: Turning around and looking the other way gives us this portrait of D822 "Hercules". It is pulling away from Basingstoke with 1O12, the 12.30 Exeter–Waterloo, again on 25 August 1971, with a neat looking rake of ten Mark 1 coaches in tow. To the left are Long Valley Sidings, which surprisingly remain in use today. Nearer the camera is the loading bank, where a lone wagon is standing. This area also survives and is now used by Network Rail as a vehicle park. Basingstoke station can be glimpsed in the far distance. Behind the fourth and fifth coaches is Basingstoke Panel Signal Box; this opened on 20 November 1966 to control the West of England Line from the west of Woking to Andover; its area of control was later extended to Grateley. From 16 April 2007 control of the route between Farnborough and Grateley passed to the new Basingstoke Area Signalling Centre (BASC). The latter, which also houses the Dorset Coast Poole to Moreton Panel, is to be found in the building on the Up side of the station adjacent to Platform 5, which is the bay normally used for services to and from Reading. The BASC is not to be confused with Network Rail's Operating Centre (ROC Wessex) which is situated in the V of the junction of the main line and that from Reading. This at present only controls some of the lines near the London end of the system; the plan is that all of the South Western system will be controlled from here, although the timescale for this is unknown. Behind the 1966 Panel Signal box and the grass bank on the right is where the former-GWR line from Reading runs into the station. One thing that has changed is Basingstoke's skyline; over the more than half a century since I stood here, the town has seen significant development, bringing a change in its character from a market town to an economic centre with many modern office blocks. I wonder how many residents of the luxury flats that now stand opposite the signal box of 1966 spend their time watching the trains go by.

Above right: The time is 10.20 and I have just alighted from 1O08, the 07.20 Exeter–Waterloo after a fine run behind D818 "Glory" which included a full English breakfast in the restaurant car. At Basingstoke, I then ran forward to grab a shot of the train before it left for the capital to find the bonus of the unique 8-VAB EMU 8001 standing beside it. This bears the headcode 92, which at the time indicated a semi-fast service on the Waterloo to Southampton, Bournemouth & Weymouth route. The unit was a one-off, formed in 1968 by joining three Class 423 4-VEP EMUs and a Mark 1 buffet car, due to a shortage of third rail electric stock when the Bournemouth line was electrified. Under the TOPS number scheme it was rebranded as a Class 480 and was then disbanded in 1974 after the stock shortage had been overcome. Two of the units reverted to their original guise and the other was used for spares. Briefly returning to the subject of Basingstoke station, which is 48 miles from Waterloo, this initially opened as a terminus when the line from Winchfield was completed on 10 June 1839. Once the line from Winchester was built it became a through station on 11 May 1840. The GWR then arrived in the town when its broad gauge line from Reading was opened 1 November 1848, terminating at a station alongside that of the L&SWR. The Gauge Commissioners ordered the GWR to install a third standard gauge rail, which was achieved on 22 December 1856 when Basingstoke became a junction; through passenger and goods services to and from the south coast could then pass without hindrance. The GWR station closed on 1 January 1932, after which all services used the by-then SR station and the GWR facility was demolished. Since the dieselisation of Waterloo to West of England services in September 1964, all trains in both directions call at Basingstoke, which like at Woking, was not the case during the era of steam.

Right: Here we can enjoy the going away view of a smart and clean looking D818 on the same train at Basingstoke, as it glistens in the morning sunshine. I will leave the reader to imagine the symphony that could be heard on its departure, as it sped away for Waterloo. Note beyond the platform the line to Reading that curves away to the left.

Left: A couple of miles west of Basingstoke the railway passes over the Roman road to Winchester before it reaches Worting Junction. There the Southampton line and the West of England route take their separate tracks before the final parting of the ways at Battledown. On 25 August 1971, D6548 and its empty Sea Cow ballast wagons, which are most likely on the first stage of their long journey to Meldon for a refill, are midway between the two locations, running on the rails of the West Country route. Note to the left of the train the Up line from Southampton dropping down from the flyover which is behind the photographer, before it joins the metals from Salisbury to form the four-track section that continues east.

Below left: The topography of the land between the junction and the flyover allowed the opportunity to obtain a decent broadside portrait of a Warship in full flight. With the Up line from Southampton visible behind the engine, as mentioned in the previous caption, D810 "Cockade" hurries along with 1V13, the 13.08 Waterloo–Exeter on 25 August 1971.

Above: Worting was originally a flat junction, but the growing levels of traffic caused congestion, as Salisbury-bound trains had to cross the line for those from Southampton. The bottleneck was overcome by the construction of Battledown Flyover, which opened on 30 May 1897; the actual meeting place of the two routes is at Worting Junction, about half a mile to the east. This powerful image is dated 25 August 1971 and shows D811 "Daring" working 1O10, the 10.10 Exeter–Waterloo, as it powers around the curve under the flyover which takes the Up line from the Southampton & Bournemouth direction over the twin tracks of the Salisbury route. The view here is similar today, but is spoilt by clutter and some vegetation growth.

Above: Not long after the previous photograph was taken, this was the view looking the other way on the same day. D812 "The Royal Naval Reserve 1859–1959" leans into the curve under the flyover, with 1V11, the 11.08 Waterloo–Exeter. The Up line from Southampton is behind the train and the Down line to the South Coast is in the foreground. Just seven years earlier, the forerunner of this service was the Down Atlantic Coast Express (ACE), the 11.00 from Waterloo. The ACE was split into nine different portions to serve a variety of destinations across the west of England. A coach was removed at Salisbury and this followed the ACE as a stopping service for the benefit of passengers travelling to the nearby local stations. Carriages for Sidmouth and Exmouth were detached at Sidmouth Junction and the restaurant car was removed at Exeter Central. There, the portions for Plymouth, Bude and Padstow were removed, to run forward as a separate train on the Okehampton line. The remaining coaches ran to Barnstaple Junction, where those for Ilfracombe and Torrington would be separated. When through services from Waterloo to the west were dieselised and rationalised from 7 September 1964, the 11.00 initially only ran to Salisbury. Here passengers continuing west had to change for the through Brighton to Plymouth service and a similar arrangement applied in the opposite direction. The train from the South Coast would already be busy and so once passengers from the South East joined at Salisbury, it was usually overcrowded. This soon led to a full in-tray for the Western Region's complaints department! As a result, common sense was restored from the start of the 1968 summer timetable, when through running to Exeter was reinstated for the appropriate trains from Waterloo. Incidentally, D812 was one of the two Western Region Warships that weren't actually named after a Warship, the other was D800 "Sir Brian Robertson", who was Chairman of the British Transport Commission between 1953 and 1961.

Below: This photograph shows that during the next 44 years not much changed at this location. On 6 April 2015, 66085 heads west under the flyover with 6V47, the 10.27 Tilbury–Margam. The freight train had been diverted this way due to engineering work that required the closure of the Great Western main line at Reading. The flyover looks smart after a repaint into green and if one looks carefully beneath it, some graffiti that vandals have left is visible.

CHAPTER 2 -
THE WEST OF ENGLAND MAIN LINE: FROM ANDOVER TO SALISBURY AND YEOVIL

Above: The L&SWR main line from Basingstoke to Salisbury opened on 3 July 1854 and its most notable feature is perhaps the Hurstbourne Viaduct between Whitchurch and Andover. The structure is 127 yards long, constructed of dark red bricks and has nine round-headed arches with a 34-foot span. It carries the railway over the B3048 to St Mary Bourne and the burbling Bourne Rivulet. A rare visitor is captured hurrying its way towards the capital (to the right), in the form of 43018, which is out of sight leading and 43024 on the rear. This is 1O43, the 10.00 Penzance–Waterloo, which instead of taking the usual route to London Paddington, was diverted east of Westbury, including this section of the former L&SWR main line. The date is 6 April 2015, when the train travelled this way because Reading station was closed due to engineering work. This and the following weekend were one of the few occasions when HSTs could be seen on the route. Note Viaduct Cottages nestling in front of the structure, which complete this sylvan scene.

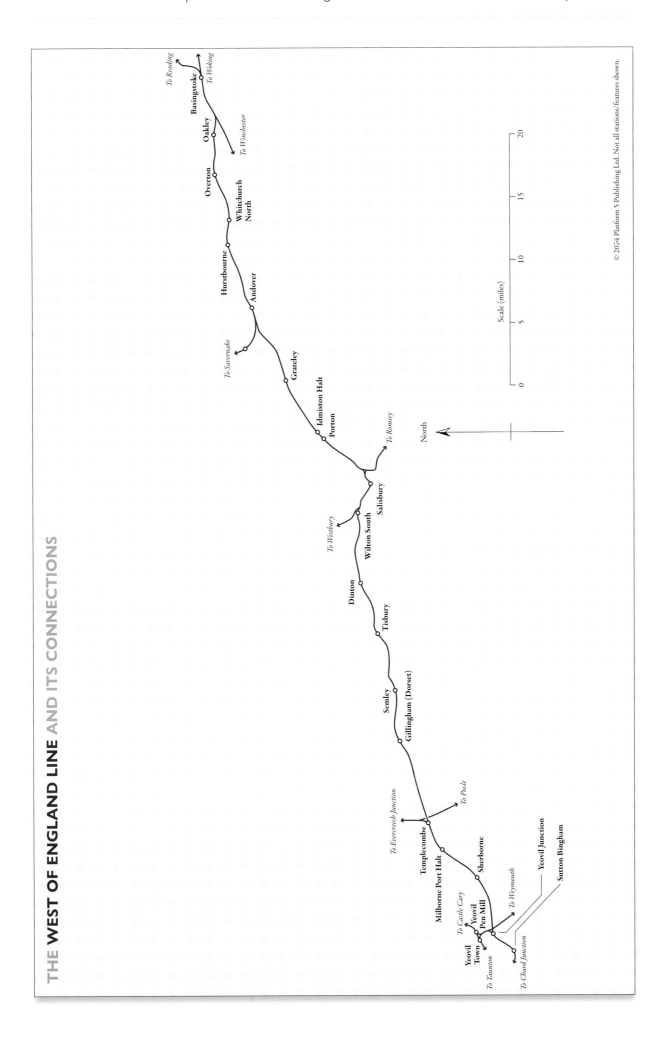

THE WEST OF ENGLAND LINE AND ITS CONNECTIONS

To Reading
Basingstoke
To Woking
Oakley
Overton
To Winchester
Whitchurch North
Hurstbourne
Andover
To Savernake
Grateley
Idmiston Halt
Porton
To Romsey
Salisbury
Wilton South
To Westbury
Dinton
Tisbury
Semley
Gillingham (Dorset)
To Evercreech Junction
To Poole
Templecombe
Milborne Port Halt
Sherborne
To Castle Cary
Yeovil Pen Mill
To Weymouth
Yeovil Town
Yeovil Junction
Sutton Bingham
To Taunton
To Chard Junction

North

Scale (miles)
0   5   10   15   20

© 2024 Platform 5 Publishing Ltd. Not all stations/features shown.

Above: We now call at Andover station, which is 66 miles from Waterloo. Here we have another rare visitor to the area, a Western Region three-car Class 119 DMU. The unit is formed of vehicles 51065, 59424 & 51093 and is working 1Z58, the 08.50 Berkshire Rambler railtour from Bristol Temple Meads. This took the participants (myself included) to Ludgershall and back on 13 November 1971. Andover station opened along with the line in 1854 and this view looks east towards Basingstoke. To the right and partially obscured by the Down platform canopy are the original L&SWR buildings of 1854, which are now Grade II listed. The station became a junction and was suitably renamed upon the opening of the branch to Romsey (Kimbridge Junction) on 6 March 1865. Its status was further enhanced with the opening of the Swindon Marlborough & Andover Railway's (SM&AR) line from Grafton in the north on 1 May 1882. In 1884 this became the southern part of the Midland & South Western Junction Railway (M&SWJR) from Cheltenham Spa, which surprisingly in the Grouping of 1923 was absorbed into the GWR. The M&SWJR route closed on 9 September 1961 and only the line between Andover and Ludgershall survives for military traffic. The Sprat & Winkle, as the more southerly line to Romsey was known, then closed to passengers on 7 September 1964 and completely on 13 September 1967. All West of England trains in each direction have called at Andover since the timetable recast of 7 September 1964. On the same day, the station reverted to its original name, being a junction no more. This view is still recognisable today, although I'm sure that passengers would no longer be allowed to stand in between the tracks to take photographs!

Above right: Continuing with the theme of rare visitors to Andover and railtours to Ludgershall, here we have a class of engine not often seen in these parts in the form of 37116 working a Basingstoke to Ludgershall shuttle on 27 September 1987. The occasion was the festivities of Basingstoke Rail Week. Around this time, the management of BR's Southern Region became very active in promoting events to raise the profile of the railway in the area. This included running exotic motive power down the freight line to Ludgershall, which was one of the crowd pullers. The other two locomotives that hauled trains to Ludgershall that day were 40122 and ex-Somerset & Dorset and LMS Class 7F 53809. With the many different companies that form today's railway, one has to wonder whether events like this will ever be staged again.

Right: After having crossed Salisbury Plain and reached the outskirts of the cathedral city, D813 "Diadem" takes the curve from the Andover direction with 1V13, the 13.10 Waterloo–Exeter on 29 April 1970. The train is passing Salisbury Tunnel Junction signal box and is about to enter the 443-yard Fisherton Tunnel. The railway in this part of Salisbury evolved in a rather roundabout way. Firstly, on 2 May 1847 the branch from Eastleigh and Romsey opened, reaching a new station called Milford to the east of the city. On 1 May 1857, the direct route from Andover opened, also travelling to the Milford terminus. Two years later, on 2 May 1859, the line from Andover was diverted onto a new alignment, on which we see D813. On the same day the line from Romsey, as seen on the right, was extended to join this new route into Salisbury, completing the above layout of Salisbury Tunnel Junction. At the same time in 1859, Milford closed to passengers (it was retained as a freight station until 1967 and little trace of it now remains) and the direct curve from the Andover direction to Milford also closed, although its formation remained intact and is visible behind the large house on the right. This curve was then re-laid 122 years later in 1981 to provide an alternative through route for the growing container traffic from Southampton. This created a complete railway triangle to the east of Salisbury for the first time. On 31 October 2021, this location made the headlines for the wrong reasons. While 158762 & 158763 were travelling slowly around the curve from Romsey (on the right) with the 16.30 Portsmouth Harbour–Cardiff, they

were struck by 159102 as it arrived on the line from Andover with the 17.20 Waterloo-Honiton. The latter had overrun a red signal due to a lack of adhesion. Both trains were derailed and whilst there were no fatalities, 13 people were injured including the driver of the 159 and the line was not reopened until 16 November 2021. Fortunately such incidents are very rare on our railways which have an excellent safety record.

Salisbury station is 83.5 miles from Waterloo and give or take a few miles, is the half way point between Waterloo and Exeter. The first station was a terminus that the GWR opened on completion of its line from Westbury on 30 June 1856. What later became the adjacent L&SWR station then opened on 2 May 1859 with the completion of the first part of the Salisbury & Yeovil Railway. This second station was located immediately south of its GWR counterpart and was operated by the L&SWR from the outset. It had a single lengthy platform and to ease the transfer of passengers between the two stations, a footbridge was provided in 1860. A second platform was added a decade later. There was much activity in enlarging the facilities as the 19th century gave way to the 20th century, with two new platforms being added

between the GWR and L&SWR stations and a subway was built, completing the layout that is broadly similar today. The GWR station then closed on 12 September 1932, when all services were transferred to the now SR station, an early and sensible example of rationalising duplicate facilities and better using manpower. The GWR trainshed was subsequently demolished; the GWR station buildings are now Grade II listed and remain in commercial use. The site of the GWR sidings and yard became the home of the Salisbury Traincare Depot when this opened on 11 June 1993 to service the Class 159 DMUs. The first of these units to enter service was 159004 on a Waterloo–Salisbury relief working on 2 March 1993. The official launch of the class was on 6 April 1993 and the last loco-hauled train on the route ran on 10 July 1993.

Below: In the days when vegetation growth was kept at bay, the A30 overbridge, which is visible in the previous photograph, provided an excellent platform for photographing trains leaving Fisherton Tunnel, which is known locally as Bishopdown Tunnel. The almost cottage-like Salisbury Tunnel Junction signal box stands on the right; this had a 21-lever frame and would close on 17 August 1981, when the Salisbury Panel took over signalling for the area. With a discernible plume of exhaust and a wonderful rendering of hydraulic music, D819 "Goliath" roars out of the tunnel working 1O12, the 12.30 Exeter–Waterloo on 29 April 1970. Note the neat and tidy allotments above the cutting, which are now obscured by a veritable forest, making a shot like this impossible.

Above: After relocating slightly to the left, Class 35 D7068 soon followed D819 with 1O63, the 12.35 Cardiff General–Portsmouth Harbour (as the former was known until its name was changed to Cardiff Central in May 1973). The Hymeks, as the class were known, were a regular sight at Salisbury at the time. They were rarely seen on the Waterloo trains, with just the odd one now and again making an appearance when a Warship failed. The Cardiff to Portsmouth and Waterloo to Exeter workings were timed to connect with each other at Salisbury in both directions. This was the era when connecting trains would be held for a reasonable amount of time for the benefit of the passengers, something that is completely overlooked by the delay-repay conscious penalty system of today's privatised railway.

Above: At Salisbury, the Up Bay (Platform 6) is an extension of the Down Main (Platform 4) at the east end of the station. Over the years this has been a popular grandstand for train spotters and photographers. There we find D827 "Kelly" at the head of 1V15, the 15.10 Waterloo–Exeter slowing for Salisbury station on 29 April 1970. I travelled on this to Exeter, enjoying a meal in the restaurant car, then went to Newton Abbot to watch on my then girlfriend's television the first FA Cup Final replay since 1912. For the record Chelsea beat Leeds United 2–1 at Old Trafford. Back to the matter in hand, between the signal at the end of the platform and Salisbury East Signal Box which is visible to its left is where the junction was for what I believe was the shortest independent railway in the country, namely the 460-yard Salisbury Railway & Market House Company. The ancient market here was owned by the citizens of the city, who foresaw the coming of the railway, but were concerned that it did not come close enough to the market. They feared this could cause a loss of trade and deter dealers who might send their produce elsewhere. With great foresight, they obtained the necessary powers to build a short line to their market and warehouses, and this opened on 24 May 1859. It was worked by the L&SWR, and subsequently by the SR and later BR, but remained independently owned. Traffic ceased in 1962 and its formal closure date was 1 July 1964. It was one of the few railways not to be acquired in the Grouping of 1923 and also had the distinction of being one of the few not to be nationalised in 1948. The company was voluntarily wound up in 1965, ending the story of this very short railway, albeit one with an important place in history. To the left of D827 is the former East Yard and sidings, which alas are also no more.

Above right: One the same day in 1970, hard on the heels of D827 came D7064 with 1V30, the 15.23 Portsmouth Harbour–Cardiff General which is displaying an incorrect headcode. Sadly, the above-mentioned 2021 incident at Salisbury Tunnel Junction was not the only serious railway accident in the area. On 1 July 1906, the driver of a boat train from Stonehouse Quay (on the short branch from the L&SWR station in Devonport) to Waterloo ignored the 30mph speed limit through the station and the east curve. The train raced through at more than double this speed and reeled on the curve, striking a westbound empty milk train in the process. This resulted in extensive damage and 28 fatalities, four of whom were train crew. It was at the height of the fierce competition between the L&SWR and the GWR for the lucrative ocean liner traffic from the Port of Plymouth. The boat trains had luxury stock and included the only sleeping cars owned and operated by the L&SWR. They were run to fast schedules and were the only trains not to call at Salisbury, although engine changes took place at Templecombe. To compound the misery for the L&SWR, on the following day the GWR opened its shortened route from Paddington to Taunton via Castle Cary, which reduced its line by 20 miles and the timings by as many minutes (GWR trains previously ran via Bristol). The battle for ocean traffic ended in 1910, as relations between the two companies improved and the L&SWR was happy to cut its losses.

Below: It is only possible to obtain a picture like this during high summer, when the sun moves far enough round to illuminate a train arriving at Salisbury from the east. Here we see D824 "Highflyer" with 1V19, the 19.08 Waterloo–Exeter on 29 May 1970, passing Class 205 1130 in Platform 6. I had obtained permission from the station staff to disobey the notice telling passengers that they must cross the line by means of the subway, so that I could jump on the back of 1V19 which would take me home after a day of photography in the New Forest area. Then followed a roast chicken dinner in the restaurant car, listening to D824 all the way to Exeter St Davids, followed by D859 "Vanquisher" forward to Plymouth on 1C01, the 21.15 Bristol Temple Meads–Plymouth. As 1C01 was a slow stopping service that usually consisted of three passenger coaches and six vans, it was unofficially known as The Parliamentary. It ran to a slow 3¼-hour schedule, but Warships and Mark 1 stock made for a very enjoyable journey, regardless of the speed.

Above: The Peaks (Classes 45 & 46) were seen occasionally at Salisbury, arriving on the line from Westbury or those from Eastleigh or Southampton. Class 45 D52 waits with 1M07, the 18.42 Portsmouth & Southsea–Derby vans on 22 May 1970. This train took an indirect route, travelling via Southampton, Salisbury and Bristol. The Peak would have taken over from a Class 33 in Northam Yard, Southampton. At the time, this duty was rostered for a Hymek and was worked by a Bristol Bath Road depot crew, so it is more than likely that the Peak was a late replacement following a Hymek failure, which sadly was not an uncommon occurrence. D52 carried the name "The Lancashire Fusilier" as it was one of 26 Peaks to be named after British army regiments and it would become 45123 a few years later under TOPS.

Above right: 47711 basks in the evening sunshine at Salisbury with 2V17, the 17.05 Waterloo–Exeter on 21 July 1992. The building seen behind the engine on Platform 3 had always intrigued me. It has featured in many photographs and publications, but no reference to its use ever seemed to be mentioned. It looks like a signal box, especially with those access steps, but recent research has revealed that it has never been a signal box. There would have been no need for a box on Salisbury's platforms, as only 38 chains separate the East and West signal boxes at either end of the station. The structure is in fact one of the station buildings from an early but unknown date. Its original purpose was to supply warming pans that passengers could carry on the trains to keep warm, as tubular foot warmers and steam heating didn't come into use until around the 1880s. During the days of locomotive-hauled trains, it was used by the shunters who were based here, and until the 1980s it also served as the Carriage & Wagon fitters mess room and store. Their workshop was on the ground floor and I am reliably informed that vices and benches remain inside the building today. Note the green bucket and brush in the foreground that have been conveniently placed for drivers to give their windscreens a wash before proceeding west; this was one of those little touches of the railway that could easily be taken for granted.

Right: The reign of the Warships on the Waterloo–Exeter route ended after they had been in charge of it for seven years and a month. The transition took place on a weekend which saw a major cull of the fleet, as BR's Western Region hastened its quest to be rid of the Hydraulics. It would however, be more than five years until this mission was accomplished, with the end for the Class 52 Westerns coming in February 1977 (the class were very rarely seen on Waterloo to West of England services). I now present two historic night portraits at Salisbury, showing the final diagrammed Warship workings on the route, both on the evening of Sunday 3 October 1971. Along with many other enthusiasts, I travelled from Exeter to Salisbury behind D823 "Hermes" on 1O18, the 18.20 Exeter–Waterloo. This arrived at 20.24 and after a quick dash through the subway with my camera already mounted on a tripod, this two minute F8 exposure was captured on 64ASA Ektachrome film. The wavy white line alongside the train is not a fault, but the mark made by the lamp of the Carriage & Wagon examiner, who would not stand still for the required exposure time, creating this evocative scene.

Above: We then returned west behind D822 "Hercules" on 1V19, the 19.08 Waterloo–Exeter. Even though this was already running late, more time was lost at Salisbury, as the very co-operative Exeter train crew made sure there was sufficient time for the photographers to take our two-minute exposures, to record the historic occasion. Can one imagine the railway staff being so helpful today? Note the lineup of Class 33s on the right, which are ready to take over on passenger services the following morning. D6535 had arrived earlier in the day on 1V09, the 09.08 from Waterloo, to provide traction for the first working out of Exeter the following morning. D822 eventually set off at 21.17, 31 minutes late, putting in a fine performance and arriving at Exeter St Davids at 23.09. As it turned out, these were not the very last hydraulic workings on the route, as we will see later in this chapter. Class 33s weren't ideal replacements for the more powerful Warships and didn't solve the problem of diesel reliability. Diesel hydraulics would be utilised on the odd occasion due to Class 33 non availability. For example, the December 1972 Railway Observer notes that on 6 October 1972 Hymek D7050 worked the 17.55 Exeter–Waterloo, which left 34 minutes late and the next day D7076 worked the Exeter to Chard Junction (and back) milk train. The following week, on 14 October 1972, due to Class 33 failures, two very rare occurrences took place; D1047 "Western Lord" worked the 06.38 Waterloo–Exeter forward from Salisbury and D832 "Onslaught" hauled the 12.25 Exeter–Waterloo, a final Warship fling one could say.

Right: This photograph could be described as a sunset on the Warship era on the West of England route. It is no longer possible to take photographs from the carriage window like this, partly because trains no longer have manually opening windows and also due to health and safety requirements. On 29 May 1970, D824 "Highflyer" heads west past the Salisbury West home signal and towards the setting sun with 1V19, the 19.08 Waterloo-Exeter. As the train and rails glint from the last rays of the sun and I head for the restaurant car, we now turn our attention to the route west to Exeter Central.

The history of the main line from Salisbury to Exeter Central is relatively straightforward. The Salisbury & Yeovil Railway's (S&YR) line between Salisbury and Gillingham opened on 2 May 1859 and was operated by the L&SWR. It was extended to Sherborne on 7 May 1860 and to Yeovil a few weeks later on 1 June 1860, where it met the GWR branch from Taunton at Hendford on the outskirts of Yeovil. On 1 June 1861, the station in Hendford (Yeovil) was superseded by the jointly owned (L&SWR and GWR) Yeovil Town station. Of Yeovil's three main stations, Town was the most conveniently located, but as BR did at other locations such as Great Yarmouth, it later closed the station with the best location during the cull of the 1960s. From a junction at Bradford Abbas, the line from Salisbury was extended to Yeovil Junction and Exeter Queen Street (the original name of Exeter Central) on 19 July 1860. The direct curve between Bradford Abbas and Yeovil Town closed on 1 January 1870, meaning that all through workings from Yeovil Town that were heading east towards Salisbury and Waterloo had to reverse at Yeovil Junction. The course of the earlier route is still discernible and the abutments of the bridge that took it over the GWR's Castle Cary to Weymouth line can be picked out from a passing train on the main line. The S&YR was taken over by the L&SWR in 1878 and the whole route passed to the SR with the 1923 Grouping. It then became part of BR's Southern Region in 1948, when little in the way of amendments to the timetable were made.

Bigger changes came from 1 January 1963, when the Southern Region lines west of Wilton South (west of Salisbury) were transferred to BR's Western Region (WR). This was a development that few had foreseen and the WR had not taken into account its unexpected inheritance of the line between Exeter and Wilton

South when planning the transition from steam to diesel. From 1963, the Waterloo to the West of England route was effectively split into two, with the Southern Region controlling the busier half between Waterloo and Salisbury, and the WR managing the western half, which included services to and from the west that terminated at Salisbury. The first major change came from 7 September 1964, when the timetable was recast. Waterloo to Exeter trains were treated as inter-regional workings, with the provision of motive power and rolling stock being the responsibility of the WR. Services to and from the east that terminated at Salisbury remained the responsibility of the Southern Region, and the Waterloo to Exeter timetable contained a footnote advising passengers to consult the Southern Region timetable for additional services between Waterloo and Salisbury. As for motive power, Waterloo to Exeter services were fully dieselised from this time, but the Southern Region continued with steam east of Salisbury, particularly on its commuter services to and from Waterloo. This continued until the end of steam on the Southern Region in July 1967. During those latter years of steam, Salisbury shed kept its stud of Bulleid Pacifics in tip top condition until the Class 42 Warships took over.

The era of diesel trains on the Waterloo to West of England services, particularly on the section between Salisbury and Exeter, can be split into fives phases. The Warships worked these from September 1964 to October 1971. Class 33s then took over until they were superseded by the more powerful Class 50s that had been displaced by the introduction of HSTs on trains from Paddington. The first day that a Class 50 operated on the line out of Waterloo was 5 November 1979 and the class took over completely with the May 1980 timetable change. Then followed the most short-lived chapter, when Class 47s began working some Exeter to Waterloo trains from 1988. The 47s shared the duties with Class 50s for a few years while the latter were gradually phased out and replaced, with the 50s holding out until early 1992. The reign of the Class 47s was therefore only for a short period. Finally, the era of the Class 159 DMUs began in 1993, with some 158s also being used in later years. At the time of writing, 30 years after their introduction, the 159s have been operating on the route for longer than the combined years of all their diesel-hauled predecessors, and a decade longer than that of the Bulleid Pacifics. During the last three decades there has been a vast increase in the number of services. There were just five daily through trains when the Warships plied their way along the route in 1964 and now there are more than triple that number. Sadly, restaurant cars are a distant memory and today's refreshment trollies with their usually not very warm tea and coffee are a poor substitute. As I write these words in 2023, no replacements for the 159s are lined up, so it seems that they will be continuing for a while yet.

Above: For trains travelling west from Salisbury, the route involves a fairly sharp climb that predominantly rises at 1 in 115. One of the great landmarks on this part of our journey is Salisbury Cathedral of the Blessed Virgin Mary, which predates the arrival of the railway in Salisbury by over 600 years. Here the cathedral, which is partially obscured by trees, forms the backdrop for a sight that is not likely to be witnessed again. 43015 approaches Wilton Road overbridge, with 43031 on the rear, forming 1V77, the 16.07 Waterloo–Penzance on 6 April 2015. Due to engineering work closing all routes through Reading station that weekend, Paddington to the West of England services were diverted to run from Waterloo to Salisbury and forward to Westbury, where they would reverse before continuing west. From this view it is difficult to believe that there used to be another double track railway in the area on the left, the GWR route to and from Salisbury which will be explained in the next caption.

Above: The GWR and SR routes used to run parallel out of Salisbury for over two miles as they headed west. The former GWR metals were taken out of use on 27 October 1973, with the exception of a lengthy siding that was retained to serve the chalk slurry depot at Quidhampton. A new junction was installed about a quarter of a mile short of the actual divergence, maintaining the four track scene which still looks much the same today. On 22 May 1970, D7004 travels towards Westbury with 1V32, the 17.23 Portsmouth Harbour–Cardiff. Note the ex-LMS parcels van behind the engine. About half a mile west of here is the starting point for one of BR's most unnecessary and shortsighted acts of rationalisation, namely the singling of the line between Salisbury and Exeter. By 1967 most of the intermediate stations had been closed, leaving only Tisbury, Gillingham, Sherborne, Yeovil Junction, Crewkerne, Axminster, Honiton and Whimple, the last of which only being served by commuter services to and from Exeter. Wilton South to Templecombe was singled with effect from 1 April 1967, with only one passing loop at Gillingham on the 26-mile stretch. Sherborne to Chard Junction followed on 7 May 1967, with no intermediate loop, not even at Yeovil Junction (although that later changed), followed by Chard Junction to Pinhoe on 21 May 1967 with a passing loop at Honiton on this 29-mile stretch. Double track was maintained between Templecombe and Sherborne with the Up line signalled as bidirectional. This all looked good on paper, with a two-hourly service and the relatively short stretch of double track gave some breathing space for late running, but the folly of this plan was soon realised when it transpired that the WR's Tokenless Block signalling system was rather temperamental and the Warships were not as reliable as expected. After many delays and much disruption, in a case of "we told you so", the second track was reinstated between Sherborne and Yeovil Junction from 1 October 1967. The restricted capacity is felt to this day, although as we shall see, there have been some improvements and station reopenings. The Yeovil Junction to Exeter section is really put to the test when GWR services are diverted that way; some Waterloo–Exeter trains have to be turned back at Yeovil Junction, although stations such as Crewkerne and Honiton benefit from being served by the diverted GWR trains to Plymouth and Penzance.

Above: About a mile east of Tisbury, in this charming pastoral location, lies Tisbury Gates where the railway crosses a minor road. There we find 47611 "Thames" hurrying through with 1O86, the 09.40 Plymouth–Brighton on 15 April 1989, nearly four years after automatic half barriers were installed at the crossing in July 1985. We are looking west along the beautiful valley of the River Nadder, which will be crossed by the railway three times in the four miles between here and Semley. There the line enters Dorset for the first time, before it flirts between Dorset and Somerset and then enters Devon between Chard Junction and Axminster. It is on this stretch of line that control of the route passes from the Salisbury Panel back to the Basingstoke Panel which controls it all the way to Pinhoe on the outskirts of Exeter.

Above right: At the same location, 47583 "County of Hertfordshire" and a neat rake of matching Network SouthEast (NSE) stock head west through the summer greenery with 1V09, the 08.35 Waterloo–Exeter on 10 June 1992. The section from Wilton South to the 117½ milepost, half a mile east of Sherborne, reverted back to BR's Southern Region in 1981, as traffic levels were growing on the route. To increase capacity, a passing loop was added to the east of Tisbury station on 24 March 1986, at a cost of £435,000. To add insult to the financial injury, the loop could not be installed at Tisbury station, as the disused trackbed had been sold, leaving no room for a second line. NSE was a product of the reorganisation of BR that took place during the 1980s. The national operator was split into sectors in 1982 and NSE was created when the London & South East sector was renamed in 1986. It was responsible for commuter and local services in the south-east of England and it radiated out as far as Chelmsford, Northampton and Oxford. The idea was to provide a uniform service and brand for all the inner and outer commuter lines to and from the capital. The 1986 launch included a distinct new brand with a red, white and blue livery. On the West of England line, its sphere of control went much further than the logical limit of Salisbury, continuing instead to Exeter. Consequently, for the first time since 1962, Waterloo to Exeter services were under the control of one organisation. The benefits of this included the extension of West of England services from Salisbury to locations such as Gillingham and Yeovil Junction. Despite the great success of this enterprise, it was disbanded on 1 April 1994 when its operations were transferred to the new Train Operating Companies created ahead of the privatisation of BR. What was largely the former L&SWR system was one of the first to be turned over to the private sector, with South West Trains taking over the running of trains from 4 February 1996.

Right: In this rural scene, 33109 & 33116 and Trailer Control (TC) set 8017 are about to reach Gillingham station with 1L07, the terminating 12.10 from Waterloo on 13 May 1989. Rather than terminating at Salisbury, these workings to Gillingham had been made possible by the installation of the loop at Tisbury. The TCs were unpowered three or four-car sets that had a driving trailer at either end. They had been converted from Mark 1 stock in conjunction with the electrification of the line to Bournemouth in 1967, for use on the line forward to Weymouth. They could work in multiple with either 4-REP EMUs, Class 33/1s or Class 73 electro-diesels. Once the work for which the TCs had been converted came to an end when the line between Bournemouth and Weymouth was electrified in 1988, they remained in use until loco-hauled services on the West of England route ended. Two sets have been preserved, one of which sees some use with London Transport. It was unusual for two Class 33s to haul a 4-TC set and the number of enthusiasts' heads protruding from the windows suggests it could be a special working. The train has just passed over the River Lodden and if it were continuing west, it would soon cross the River Stour.

Above: Gillingham station in Dorset (as opposed to the station of the same name in Kent) is 105 miles from London Waterloo. There we see 50023 "Howe" departing with 1V11, the 11.10 Waterloo–Exeter on 13 May 1989, which was only a couple of weeks after the station had celebrated its 130th anniversary. It is conveniently situated for the town and is notable for the blue plaque that is displayed there which reads "On 3 September 1856 near this spot, the Hon Miss Seymour cut the first turf for the Salisbury & Yeovil Railway opened 2 May 1859". The modern looking signal box on the right opened on 28 April 1957 and survives as a ground frame to control access to the now infrequently-used sidings.

Above right: "The Brightons at Buckhorn" would be a suitable heading for these next two pictures. To the west of Gillingham, the line makes a 2.5-mile climb at 1 in 130, which steepens to 1 in 100 through Blackmore Vale, to the summit 350 feet above sea level at Buckhorn Weston. From a very convenient road overbridge where two country roads meet, 50003 "Temeraire" is captured heading west with 1V12, the 09.05 Brighton–Plymouth on 5 August 1989. This has been a popular location for photographers over the years and is still worth a visit, preferably when there is something of greater interest than the endless diet of Class 159 DMUs that pass through.

Right: Turning around and looking in the other direction sees 50049 "Defiance" having just emerged from the 742-yard Buckhorn Weston Tunnel with 1O86, the 09.33 Plymouth–Brighton on the same day. For trains heading towards Salisbury this is the summit of a five-mile climb at 1 in 90 and 1 in 100 from Templecombe. Buckhorn Western is the only tunnel and major engineering feat of the Salisbury & Yeovil Railway. Its construction was not easy for the engineers due to the geology of the Oxford Clay and water which at times has proved troublesome for those maintaining the railway. As for through trains between Plymouth and Brighton, despite there being a known traffic flow from the South East Coast to the South West, for reasons best known to the Department for Transport such services were a casualty of railway sectorisation and privatisation.

Above: 50010 "Monarch" approaches the summit of the 1 in 100 climb from Templecombe, which is marked by the 113½ milepost from Waterloo, with 1V09, the 09.10 Waterloo–Exeter on 4 October 1986. The colours of NSE have yet to make an appearance on the train, but it won't be long before Large Logo livery locos and blue and grey rakes of Mark 1 stock like this give way to the brighter new colours. The train has just entered Somerset and is running on the double track section between Templecombe and Yeovil Junction, which is one of the few places where the route still looks like a double track main line. It is travelling on the Up line which is signalled for bi-directional working. The Salisbury to Exeter line runs in an east to west direction, which is against the grain of the valleys. With a couple of exceptions, it has to bisect valleys rather than travel along them and so has become affectionately known as "The Mule", with its seesaw of inclines and descents. These begin with the climb to Semley, mostly at 1 in 115, before there's a 1 in 100 dip to Gillingham, then a rise to Buckhorn Western where the line then swoops down at 1 in 90/100 to Templecombe, for yet another rise to Milborne Port as depicted above. After a short level stretch, it's 1 in 80 down to Sherborne, then a gentle slope which extends to just beyond Yeovil Junction, where the climbing starts again at 1 in 150/140 for 4 miles. This steepens to 1 in 80 for the three miles on to the summit at the west end of Crewkerne Tunnel, where begins a 12-mile gentle descent to almost reach the sea near Seaton Junction, before the line travels inland to Honiton Bank.

Above right: Oborne Bank is not very well known and has tended to have been overlooked by the railway photographic community. In the days of steam, its formidable one mile-long 1 in 80 grade would have been challenging when making a standing start from Sherborne. The best angles of the incline are for Down trains, during the evening when the sun has moved round far enough. Not far beyond the summit at Milborne Port, in the early evening autumn sunshine 50050 "Fearless" is seen drifting down the bank with a mixed livery rake of stock in the early days of NSE, with 1V15, the 15.10 Waterloo–Exeter on 11 October 1986. The gradient is clearly visible from this angle.

Right: Moving down the bank about a half a mile, just before more level ground is reached by Sherborne Castle, the wide open countryside presents some good opportunities for railway photography. Passing Blackmarsh Farm is 47715 "Haymarket", which still bears the name that it acquired when it wore ScotRail livery and resided north of the border. It is hauling 1V16, the 16.35 Waterloo–Yeovil Junction on 10 June 1992. Behind the photographer is a large tree, the road from Sherborne and then a rising field which is the location from which the next two images were taken.

Opposite page: These two photos were taken from the aforementioned field while I waited for a steam-hauled special from Exeter on 28 June 1992. The vehicles belonging to some other photographers can be seen parked up on the B3145. The elevated view captures the long and gentle curve at the foot of the bank in its pleasant rural setting. Matching engines and coaches looked the part in NSE livery, especially when captured travelling through wide open spaces such as this. Firstly, 47711 is slowing for the approach to Sherborne station with 1V15, the 14.40 Waterloo–Exeter. Looking in the other direction, we again see 47715 heading east with 1O39, the 15.43 Exeter–Waterloo. Standing out on the ridge behind the train are the remains of Sherborne Old Castle, the ruins of a Norman castle that was once the residence of Sir Walter Raleigh and where it is believed he smoked his first pipe. Sherborne took the side of the Royalists in the English Civil War and the castle paid a heavy price for such loyalty to the Crown. To cut a long story short, once the Parliamentarians had captured it for the second time, it was slighted in October 1645 and left as a ruin, no doubt a measure to keep the people of the town in order. It now stands in the grounds of what is known as Sherborne New Castle and both are Grade I listed.

Above: The Class 205 (3H) Hampshire units were introduced in September 1957 and became known as "Thumpers" due to the distinctive sound their engines made. As the Hampshire name implies, they were put to work on local services to destinations that included Basingstoke, Andover Junction and Salisbury. They rarely strayed west of Salisbury though until the NSE era. After the line to East Grinstead was electrified in 1987, four of the similar 1962-built Class 207 (3D) Oxted units that had been used on the non-electrified lines in the South East sector were transferred to Eastleigh to replace those that contained asbestos. During that later chapter in the units' lives, on 31 May 1990, 207013 looks smart in the evening sunshine as it arrives at Sherborne station, 118 miles from Waterloo, with the 16.32 Southampton–Yeovil Junction. It is displaying headcode 44 which was used for Portsmouth Harbour to Salisbury stopping services via Netley. Its foray west of Salisbury is to provide a connection with a terminating service from Waterloo. The tenure of the Class 207s on the West of England Line would only last for six years until the beginning of the Class 159 era.

Left: Two trains pass each other on the double track section between Sherborne and Yeovil Junction that was reinstated in October 1967. The location is Bradford Abbas, as seen from Back Lane bridge, a mile to the east of Yeovil. 50041 "Bulwark" is approaching with 1V11, the 11.15 Waterloo–Exeter on 5 August 1989. The eastbound train is shown in the next photograph.

Above: This was a close encounter of the 50 kind. As 50009 "Conqueror" was rapidly filling the camera's viewfinder with 1O37, the 12.28 Exeter–Waterloo, I could hear the train from Waterloo approaching from the other direction and praying that the view of 50009 would not be "photobombed." My prayer was answered, but this is the risk that one takes when photographing trains on the far line, with the track for the other direction in the foreground. This double track section will have prevented many a delay that would have occurred if it was singled like much of the rest of the route. Note the standard Exmouth Junction Concrete Works permanent way hut on the right.

Above: Yeovil Junction is 123 miles from Waterloo. This picture from the Warship era oozes nostalgia, as the only thing that had changed since the steam era is the engine on the train. D808 "Centaur" arrives with 1V64, the Sundays 10.54 Waterloo–Exeter on 17 July 1966. It is passing a landmark which had hardly changed since the enlargement works were completed here by the L&SWR in 1909, the beautiful signal gantry that controls the station's eastern exit. From left to right, two of its six arms are for the Up bay, two are for the Up platform line and two are for the Up through, the lower arm being for the northern curve towards Pen Mill station and the upper one for the main line to Sherborne. How different it would look 12 months later. The folly of singling the Salisbury to Exeter route was particularly felt at Yeovil Junction after a seven-month period of upheaval in 1967. Sherborne to Chard Junction was singled from 7 May 1967, leaving only the former Up platform at Yeovil Junction that could be used by main line trains. The rationalisation left the farcical situation of Yeovil Junction A Signal Box controlling the curve towards Pen Mill and the entrance to the Up Yard, but the signalman had no control over the main line trains that passed his signal box. To allow movements onto the Pen Mill spur, the former SR goods yard on the Up side and the Engineers' Sidings on the Down side which are visible on the right, east and west ground frames were installed from 7 May 1967. Signalling this situation could be complicated, because the tokenless block system meant that nothing could access the single track main line if it was occupied anywhere between Sherborne and Chard Junction. That was the theory at least. I recall a manager telling me how an engine had come over from the Down Yard at the same time as another one was required to rescue a Warship that had expired on the single line. His words were "We had a Class 08 shunter go onto the single line section and it came out as a Hymek, so don't ask any more questions!" To provide some relief to all of this, Sherborne to Yeovil Junction was re-doubled from 1 October 1967, but only as far as Yeovil Junction A Signal Box. Only the former Up platform was available for passenger trains. The situation was eased from 26 March 1975, when the Up bay platform, which couldn't previously be accessed from the Exeter direction, was converted to a through platform and the double track section from A Signal Box was extended into the station.

Below: The view at Yeovil Junction 27 years later is barely recognisable. All main line trains use the former Up side of the station and both platforms are signalled so that they are bidirectional. The old and the new are side by side on 1 September 1993, with the very new 159020 in its attractive NSE livery departing with the 18.30 to Salisbury and 33008 "Eastleigh" beside it. The 33 also bears its original number, D6508, and is standing on what was the former Down through line, in the area that had originally been retained for engineering use. The station is one of two that still serve the town, Pen Mill being some two miles distant. Curiously, until 1991 when the county boundaries were altered, Yeovil Junction lay within Dorset despite the town being in Somerset, but both stations are now in Somerset. Like the other signal boxes between Gillingham and Pinhoe that survived the earlier rationalisation, the former A Box closed for good in March 2012, when the Basingstoke Panel assumed control. Today Yeovil Junction is one of the busiest stations between Salisbury and Exeter.

Above: Two stalwarts from different eras of the Waterloo to Exeter main line stand side by side at Yeovil Junction on 11 October 1986. A surprising survivor of the 1960s rationalisation was Yeovil Junction's turntable which is located on the Down side at the Exeter end of the station. It had been retained for turning engineering stock and was one of two factors that brought about the return of steam to the route that month, the other being that railtours could use the former Down platform and stable out of the way of main line trains. This was the first steam train to revisit Yeovil, with Merchant Navy Class 35028 "Clan Line" taking over from 33007 at Salisbury on the inaugural "Blackmore Vale Express" which originated at Waterloo. As 35028 slowly approached the turntable, 50045 made a timely appearance as it departed Yeovil Junction with 1V09, the 09.10 Waterloo–Exeter. In 1993 BR wished to remove the turntable, which caused an outcry leading to the formation of the Yeovil Railway Centre. The Group succeeded in retaining the turntable which is still used to turn visiting steam engines and is demonstrated during open days. The former GWR Clifton Maybank Goods Shed opposite the station has also been restored. This was accessed by a spur off the GWR's Yeovil Pen Mill to Weymouth route which now forms part of the centre's running line. A visit to the Yeovil Railway Centre is recommended.

Above right: The Class 52 Westerns were rarely seen east of Yeovil Junction (on the West of England Line), although the odd one did make it as far as Salisbury from Exeter. As far as it is known, none ever made it all the way to Waterloo. This one had travelled from Basingstoke, so the section between there and Salisbury was therefore very rare track for the class. The occasion was Tour 52, which was organised by BR management at Plymouth after approaches from the Plymouth Railway Circle. The charter was hauled throughout by D1010 "Western Campaigner" on 27 November 1976, running as 1Z52, the 07.45 from Plymouth to Birmingham New Street via Bristol and Cheltenham. It returned from the Midlands via Oxford, Reading and Basingstoke, before it returned to Plymouth via Exeter St Davids. The constraints of the single line have already been mentioned, but good use was made of this as the train had a booked 20 minute stop (18.05 to 18.25) at Yeovil Junction, where it is seen waiting for an Up train to clear the single line. The tripods therefore came out for this one and only chance to record a Western at Yeovil Junction by night.

Right: What could be more evocative than the aura of a Class 52 Western glowing in the peaceful atmosphere of a wayside station beside the platform's canopy, as its Maybach engines simmered away before it headed off into the night? It was indeed an atmosphere and a memory to be savoured. This was certainly the last Class 52 to be seen east of Yeovil Junction on the main line from Salisbury. It wasn't the last Class 52 to pass through here though; from information supplied by Tony Wardle, on the same night D1023 worked the 22.10 Penzance–Paddington, which was diverted via Honiton and Yeovil Pen Mill and early on the following morning (a Sunday), D1070 passed through with the 23.25 Paddington–Newton Abbot newspapers. The next Sunday, 5 December 1976, D1048 came this way with the diverted 07.30 Plymouth–Edinburgh, which it worked as far as Bristol and D1058 was also noted on the 15.10 Paignton–Paddington. The last known appearance of a Western on the line was an unidentified one that was heard passing through Exmouth Junction at 02.45 with the 22.10 Penzance–Paddington sleepers on 8 December 1976. As a matter of interest, in the days before the digital revolution, the exposure for this picture on 64 ASA Ektachrome film was 75 seconds at f8, and no one dared to walk in front of the tripod!

CHAPTER 3 -
THE WEST OF ENGLAND MAIN LINE: FROM YEOVIL TO EXETER CENTRAL

Above: Two miles to the east of Crewkerne, on 3 July 1988, 50001 "Dreadnought" is seen on the long straight section near North Perrot with 1O53, the 14.32 Exeter–Waterloo. This was a fortunate picture, as the sun was playing hide and seek, but emerged just as the train approached, providing the dramatic backlit conditions that photographers dream of. This does not often happen though and my experience is that the sun normally appears as the tail lamp goes by! We had taken our lunchtime subsistence in the curiously-named pub in the nearby village of Halstock – The Quiet Woman. Sadly this is no longer in business and it has become a guest house.

THE WEST OF ENGLAND LINE AND ITS CONNECTIONS

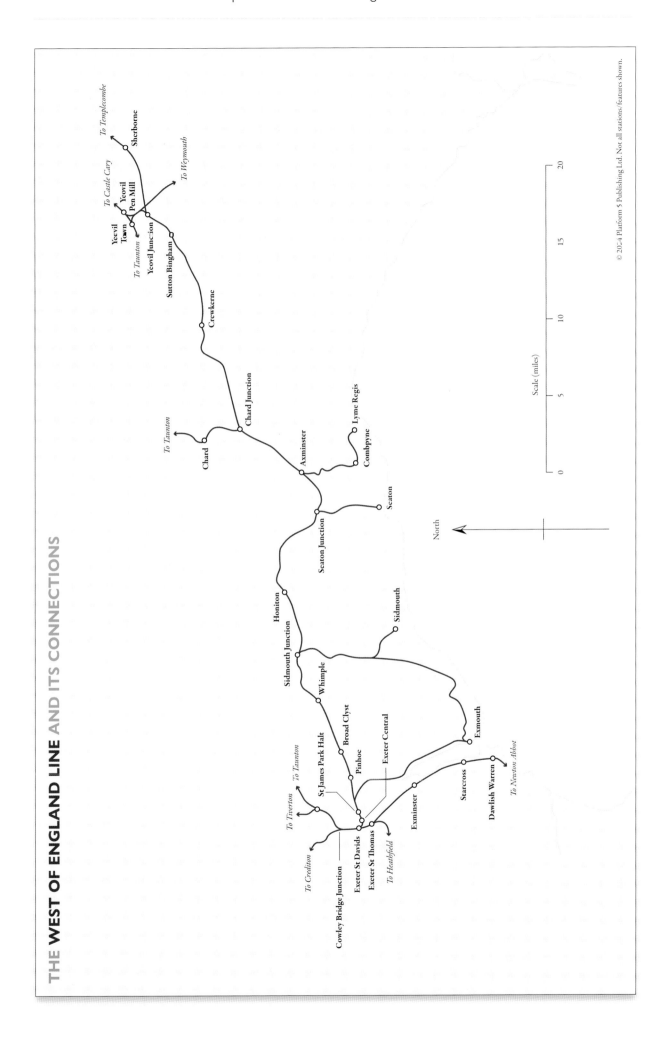

To Templecombe

Sherborne

To Castle Cary

Yeovil
Pen Mill

To Weymouth

Yeovil
Town

To Taunton

Yeovil Junction

Sutton Bingham

Crewkerne

Chard Junction

To Taunton

Chard

Axminster

Lyme Regis

Combpyne

Seaton

Seaton Junction

Honiton

Sidmouth Junction

Sidmouth

Whimple

Broad Clyst

St James Park Halt

Pinhoe

Exeter Central

To Tiverton

To Taunton

Exminster

Starcross

Dawlish Warren

To Newton Abbot

Exmouth

To Crediton

Cowley Bridge Junction

Exeter St Davids

Exeter St Thomas

To Heathfield

North

Scale (miles)

0   5   10   15   20

Above: At Crewkerne classic L&SWR architecture is on offer on the former Up platform. The building, which is 131.75 miles from Waterloo, was designed by William Tite and opened along with the line between Yeovil Junction and Exeter on 19 July 1860. The station is located a mile south of Crewkerne, near the village of Misterton and note its signature neat row of seven chimney pots. In the background is the modern-looking signal box, which opened on 6 November 1960, and the redundant goods shed. The signal box had a working life of less than seven years, closing on 26 February 1967 as a precursor to the singling of the track through here. On 27 March 2011, 43174 (front) and 43012 climb the 1 in 80 gradient with 1C84, the diverted 12.30 Paddington–Penzance. High Speed Trains (HSTs) were never employed on Waterloo–Exeter workings, so they only made infrequent appearances here when trains were diverted via Yeovil. The station has become a busy railhead that serves a wide area. Like all the surviving stations between Salisbury and Exeter, it now enjoys its best ever service to and from the capital, with as many as 15 daily trains to Waterloo. This compares extremely favourably to the timetable of the five-day working week during the preceding steam age, when during 1964 for example, there were only three daily trains.

Above right: On 27 July 1991, 50030 "Repulse" brings 1V15, the 15.15 Waterloo–Exeter past the superb location that I have always known as Crewkerne Vale. To be precise, thanks to information supplied by Crewkerne resident David Tozer, this point is 131 miles and 60 chains from Waterloo and on the lengthy 60-chain radius curve between Crewkerne station and Crewkerne Gates level crossing. The crossing is 22 chains beyond here and was converted to automatic half barrier operation on 1 November 1967. This pleasant backlit rural scene is only available during the early evenings of the summer months, when the sun has moved round this far. The view hasn't changed much over the last 30 years, but that is liable to change, as planning permission has recently been granted to build housing on the splendid field to the right of the train.

Right: A tight squeeze through the foliage was needed to reach this point above the western portal of the 205-yard Crewkerne Tunnel. It wasn't difficult to reach though, as it's accessible from the B3165, which connects Crewkerne and Lyme Regis. 33101 is working 5O18, the empty stock 12.05 Newton Abbot–Yeovil Junction, which will then form a Waterloo bound service on 14 April 1974. The train is at the summit of the climb from Axminster and could be heard long before it became visible. During the steam days, this point gave the firemen that travelled in both directions a welcome rest. If heading west, this is the start of the 13-mile 1 in 60 descent through the Axe Valley, the river valley being the only one that the Salisbury to Exeter route follows for any considerable distance. Crewkerne Tunnel serves as an example of how the Victorian railway builders took advantage of recycling. The clay excavated to create this cutting was used to make the bricks for the tunnel, which were fired on site. There was a landslide here in October 2021 and work to stabilise the cutting was only completed as recently as November 2023, when the line between Yeovil Junction and Axminster was closed for five days to allow this and other engineering work to take place.

Above: The hydraulic era returned to part of the route on Easter Sunday, 14 April 1974, when the GWR main line through Taunton was closed for engineering work. Some Paddington to the West of England services were diverted via Yeovil, with the number of these being limited by the constraints of the single line. This brought the rare appearance of one of the most iconic classes to the route that we are following. The Class 52 Westerns were sleek and fine looking engines that made a sound like no other. They all carried names with the prefix Western, many of which had a noble or military connection, and they oozed individuality and grandeur. In my view, they were cast aside well before their time. The class had a following without equal and even though only seven have been preserved, they still captivate the imagination today. Before it became famous for being the last of its class to be overhauled at Swindon Works and one of the final locos to hold out until February 1977, a very smart looking D1023 "Western Fusilier" heads 1B06, the 08.45 Paddington–Plymouth. From London this service was routed via Bristol, where a reversal was necessary, before it continued via Castle Cary, Yeovil and Exeter. It is seen close to the former Cistercian Forde Abbey near Chard, which is now a tourist attraction. The trees here have grown very large, rendering this view now impossible.

Below: Not long after D1023 had been photographed, D1067 "Western Druid" appeared from the opposite direction after it had passed D1023 at Chard Junction. This is 1A35, the 10.05 Penzance–Paddington, again on 14 April 1974. The position of the sun made this a difficult angle, but one which highlights two features worth mentioning. Firstly, the track formation shows evidence that this was once a double track main line and secondly, the line of telegraph poles. These were the bane of many a lineside photographer. We moaned about them at the time, but in retrospect they were very much part of the railway scene, a feature from the steam era that was taken for granted. They are now a rarity, having been replaced by lineside cabling or more modern technology. So much has changed on our railways over the years.

Left: This photograph enables us to literally reflect on the Warship era along the Waterloo to Exeter route. On the right, D811 "Daring" rolls through Chard Junction, which is 139.75 miles from Waterloo, with 2C58, the 06.52 Salisbury–Exeter. It is passing D818 "Glory" on 1O08, the 07.20 Exeter–Waterloo on 25 August 1971. Chard Junction was the interchange where the line to Chard began. From 1 January 1917 the passengers that alighted there (mostly from the stopping services that followed the expresses) would probably have been surprised to find a GWR train waiting in the adjacent platform to take them the 3.25 miles to Chard Central. This was after the L&SWR and the GWR found peace with other, due to the need for economies coupled with a shortage of manpower during the First World War. The GWR took over operation of the branch, with its workings effectively cut into two; trains from Taunton terminated at Chard Central and those to and from Chard Junction were operated as a separate shuttle. The last train of the day from Chard Junction travelled through to Taunton, to return the train and crew to Taunton for the night. Passenger services on the line between Chard Junction and Chard ended on 10 September 1962 and the branch to Chard Town closed when goods traffic ended on 18 April 1966. Chard Junction was then a junction no more and it closed to passengers on 7 March 1966, along with many of the smaller stations between Salisbury and Exeter. Milk traffic from the dairy beside the former Chard Junction then continued until March 1980 and the last railway staff at this location, namely the signalmen, lost their work when the Basingstoke Panel took over in 2012.

Above: Axminster is well-known for its carpets, with the carpet factory being located beside the railway at the west end of the station. This was the view from the B6231 road bridge on 4 May 1991, as 50037 "Illustrious" rolls into Axminster with 1V15, the 15.15 Waterloo–Exeter. The station is 144.75 miles from Waterloo and opened with the line on 19 July 1860. When the line between Chard Junction and Pinhoe was singled in 1967, Axminster station was left with just one track alongside its lengthy Down platform. Much has altered since then and this is one of the few places on the route that we are following where the railway infrastructure has changed for the better. In the first decade of the 21st century, following increasing passenger numbers and demand, South West Trains and Network Rail identified the need for an hourly service in each direction between Waterloo and Exeter. The constraints of the single line here meant that this was not possible, but it was achieved at huge expense when in February 2009 work started on a three-mile loop between the newly-created Axminster East and West Junctions, to the west of Chard Junction. The improvements included reinstating Axminster's Up platform with the addition of a new footbridge and lifts. The work was completed in December 2009 and the hourly service took effect with the summer 2010 timetable. This is therefore a rare example of when 1960s rationalisation was reversed. It is also worth mentioning that I have found the station cafe here to be excellent!

Above: This view from the A35 on 7 September 1991 brings us 50030 "Repulse" on 1V15, the 15.15 Waterloo–Exeter. It is pulling away from Axminster station, which is hidden by the vegetation behind the rear of the train. Axminster was once the junction for Lyme Regis. Just behind the last coach, the abutment of the bridge that carried the Lyme Regis branch over the main line is visible; its rising embankment stands out to the left of the rear coaches. The Lyme Regis branch is famed for its tight curves, severe gradients and the Adams Radial tank engines that ran from a bay platform on the Up side of Axminster station. As branch lines go, it was relatively short-lived, with a life of just 62 years. It opened on 24 August 1903 and closed on 29 November 1965, when I was on the final train. As explained in the caption for the above picture of 50037 entering Axminster's station, the view here has changed for the better with a double track railway now forming the extended loop of 2009.

Above right: This nice clear view is from the latter days of locomotive-hauled trains on the route, when anything and everything was used to keep the trains running during a period of motive power problems. 33101 has what is best described as BR General Grey livery for Departmental and Civil Engineer duties, and is working 1O43, the 17.35 Paignton–Waterloo on 24 May 1992. It is slowing for Axminster station, as the train ascends the modest 1 in 240 gradient at this point. Today the view here is of the double track line that heads towards Axminster West Junction and the trains are an endless procession of Class 159 DMUs.

Right: This colourful scene is at Whitford, just east of Seaton Junction, where 47703 "The Queen Mother" is seen in charge of 1V09, the 09.15 Waterloo–Exeter on 7 September 1991. It is approaching the curve that takes the train away from the Axe Valley, where passengers get their only glimpse of the sea, which is about three miles distant. The Salisbury to Exeter line is an inland railway and this is the only location where it comes anywhere near the coast. Passengers travelling further west on the former Southern Railway's route would have to travel many more miles before they would see the sea again. Sadly this view is now obscured due to vegetation growth.

Left: The railway passes close to Whitford, but the village's small size and proximity to Seaton Junction station meant that it was denied its own station. The deep cutting is a noticeable feature of where see 47581 heading towards the Axe Valley with 1O37, the Sundays only 11.05 Plymouth–Waterloo on 28 June 1992. If only the train could have come up via Okehampton!

Above: Continuing west from Axminster, the next station is the impressive Seaton Junction, which is 147 miles from Waterloo. It was opened as Colyton, when the main line through here opened on 19 July 1860. This photograph looks towards Exeter, with a local DMU having arrived on 3 March 1966, which was during the last week of the station's life. Note the other DMU in the curved bay platform on the left, which will form the next train for Seaton. The station became Colyton Junction on 16 March 1868, with the opening of the Seaton branch and was renamed Seaton Junction on 1 September 1869. This later layout came about when the SR rebuilt the station so it had four through lines. The work was carried out between 1927 and 1928, with the footbridges being constructed from the produce of Exmouth Junction Concrete Works. The station and the Seaton branch both closed on 7 March 1966, as part of a wider cull of many local stations. The line to Seaton was busy during the summer season, but not sufficiently so for it to avoid being on Dr Beeching's hit list. Even though Beeching left BR in 1965 to return to ICI, the Labour government that in its 1964 election manifesto had promised to end railway closures, simply carried on with them. Freight facilities at Seaton Junction were withdrawn on 18 April 1966 and its goods yard closed when coal traffic ceased on 8 May 1967. Further changes came when the route from Chard Junction to Honiton was singled and Seaton Junction's signal box closed on 11 June 1967, leaving only the Up through line. A ground frame was added to control access to the Express Dairies sidings, which provided much lucrative milk traffic for BR until this ceased in June 1973.

Above: How the scene has changed at the closed Seaton Junction by 28 June 1992. This view also looks towards Exeter and was captured from the road bridge to the east of the station, as the platform could no longer be accessed. 47583 "County of Hertfordshire" rushes through what remains of the station with 1O38, the 14.28 Exeter–Waterloo. The main station buildings on the former Up platform survive today and are in private hands. Similarly, the concrete footbridge remains and carries a public footpath. The Colyton to Seaton section of the former Seaton branch is now occupied by the Seaton Tramway, which is well worth a visit, even though it is far from any railway access. This photograph shows how the station was located in a very rural area. Let your eyes drift towards the red brick building between the trees on the right, at which we will take a close look in the next photograph.

Above right: Seaton Junction was an isolated station situated south of the hamlet of Shute, which lays claim to being the smallest village in England. Local traffic to and from the station was sparse. Like so many other railway stations both open and closed, there was the pub outside it, in this case the Shute Arms. It provided refreshments for railway staff, passengers and other passing trade and is seen on 27 July 1991, some 25 years after the adjacent station closed. As the railways contracted, so did the businesses that relied on the trade the trains brought, and the pub by the station was no exception. I enjoyed many a fine ale and good food here, often in the company of fellow photographers, as once the intended photograph had been taken, we knew we had at least 20 minutes before the next train, due to the constraints of the single line here. A combination of there being no railway staff or passengers to serve, rail enthusiasts no longer having much reason to visit and the lack of passing trade eventually took its toll. The pub closed in 2007 and has since been converted into flats. This is a good example of how decline eventually sets in once a locality's railway is withdrawn or its station is closed.

Right: What better place to stop, on the way home after spending the day photographing a Class 33 on a series of shuttle trains on the Weymouth Harbour Tramway, than Seaton Junction? It wasn't far off the A35, giving me an excuse for a meal at the Shute Arms and to record a little bit of history too. This was the period of transition from locomotive-hauled trains to Class 159 Sprinters. It was not a sudden or overnight change ahead of the last such train which ran in July 1993. Here we see 47703 "The Queen Mother" passing through Seaton Junction on 2 April 1993 with 1V15, the 15.15 Waterloo–Exeter. This was the final time this Saturday train was locomotive-hauled.

Above: After seeing "The Queen Mother" at Seaton Junction, here is another celebrity passing through in some lovely spring evening light. 50007 "Sir Edward Elgar" is hauling 1O41, the 16.22 Exeter–Basingstoke on 30 March 1991. After carrying the name "Hercules" for nearly six years, in February 1984 the engine was repainted into this green livery at Laira depot and named "Sir Edward Elgar" to mark the 50th anniversary of the death of the celebrated composer. One may ask why 50007 was chosen. There is a clue in the number, as GWR Castle Class 4-6-0 7005, which was for many years a resident of Worcester shed (85A) in the area associated with Sir Edward, also bore the composer's name. The steam engine's number is almost an anagram of its diesel predecessor. 50007 went on to become the flagship engine of BR's Western Region, particularly during the 1985 celebrations that marked the 150th anniversary of the incorporation of the Great Western Railway. In the era of sectorisation 50007 became a Network SouthEast locomotive. Chris Green, who was in charge of NSE, allowed it to remain in this livery rather than the red white and blue colours of the sector as a thank you and morale booster for Laira's staff who had kept the Class 50s in fine fettle for so long.

Above right: The bridge from which 50007 was captured carries a public footpath over the railway at Seaton Junction. It has been a favoured spot for many a railway photographer, as it offers splendid views of a trains travelling through a rural setting. On 24 May 1992, 33102 & 33002 were specially turned out as part of a mini gala to mark the forthcoming end of loco-hauled trains on the route and are seen hurrying east with 1O38, the 14.28 Exeter–Waterloo. They are descending the easy going 1 in 300 gradient, but as the line curves away out of sight behind the train, there is a noticeable difference in the gradient at the start of Honiton Bank. This peaceful scene makes it difficult to imagine the number of tracks that were here until the late 1960s. In the foreground, the remains of platforms indicate that this was the site of the junction for the Seaton branch, with the remnant of the curved branch platform on the far left. On the other side of the tracks is where the Up sidings and the rails from the dairy were; the site is now fenced off and has passed into commercial use. The area to the left of the coaches is where the Down sidings were. Further vegetation growth during the 30+ years since this view was captured means that opportunities for photographs here are now much more limited.

Right: This colourful rural scene is a little further west of Seaton Junction. 47712 "Lady Diana Spencer" has recently been overhauled and repainted from ScotRail livery into the red colours of BR's Parcels Sector. It is running 35 minutes late with 1V11, the 11.15 Waterloo–Exeter on 19 October 1991, providing an example of the frequent delays caused by the constraints of the single line. The location is Easy Bridge, where the line joins the valley of the Umborne Brook, the babbling waters of which we see in the foreground, before it joins the River Coly, a tributary of the River Axe. This is where one of the most well-known railway inclines begins; Honiton Bank is an almost five-mile climb, mostly at 1 in 80, which follows the course of the stream towards Honiton Tunnel. During the steam era, a westbound train that stopped at Seaton Junction would not have much of a run at the bank, requiring a strenuous effort for both the fireman and his machine.

Above: A rarely photographed angle is that from Colhayne Farm, near the village of Umborne, about a mile up the line from Easy Bridge. It's a tricky location for light, because for most of the day the trains are heading uphill in a more or less northerly direction, meaning that one would be shooting into the sun. I therefore chose a hazy day for this one, where we see the Class 50 that is often regarded as the one that was unfortunate not to escape the scrap man. 50046 "Ajax" heads up the 1 in 80 grade with 1V13, the 13.15 Waterloo–Exeter on 27 July 1991. The Umborne Brook is hidden by the trees above the loco. The little stream travelling through a wide valley in East Devon completes this idyllic view of a "proper train" making its way to Exeter. Could one ask for any more?

Above right: While making the merciless 1 in 80 climb, we find a rare visitor at a well-known spot. This is Wilmington, seen from the overbridge of a minor road off the A35. The railway is about to leave the wide valley of the Umborne Brook, having crossed the watercourse about a mile further down the bank. Peaks were seldom seen on passenger trains anywhere along the route between Salisbury and Exeter. This is 45111 "Grenadier Guardsman", the former D65 and the date is 14 April 1974. It is hauling 1V72, the 08.40 Leeds–Penzance, which was the only daytime westbound cross-country service to be diverted via Yeovil that day, as a result of the Easter Sunday engineering work on the GWR main line.

Right: Here we see rather more traditional fare in the spring colours at Wilmington on 30 March 1991. 50027 "Lion" ascends the incline with 1V10, the Saturdays only 11.14 Southampton–Plymouth. There is more foliage at this location today, but the view of a train climbing the bank like this is still available. That cannot be said for the other direction, which we will examine in the next image.

Above: At the same place, on same day in 1974, we find another rare visitor to the line between Yeovil and Exeter. D1057 "Western Chieftain" rolls down the bank at Wilmington with 1A49, the diverted 12.05 Penzance–Paddington. At the time, one could make out in the far background the curve that took the line left to pass the isolated Honiton Incline signal box. The view from this location now is best described as one through a never ending avenue of trees! One landmark that passengers can still observe, as they come up the bank and look to the right through the odd gap in the foliage, is the Stockland Hill mast of 1961 construction, which beams out television to the people of East Devon.

Right: This is a combination to delight those of a Hydraulic persuasion. D7044 & D820 "Grenville" toil up the 1 in 80 incline, with not far to go before they enjoy some respite from the gradient, hauling 1V09, the 40-minute late running 09.08 Waterloo–Exeter on 21 November 1970. The Hymek had been attached at Yeovil Junction to assist the ailing Warship. The delay threw the single line timetable into disarray, which sadly was not an uncommon occurrence at the time. The train is approaching Honiton Tunnel and the cutting here has had problems in recent times. A combination of excessive rain, several nearby natural springs and drainage problems have led to there being landslips. One such incident resulted in a five-day closure of the line between 19 and 23 September 2022, so that earthwork stabilisation and strengthening works could be completed. The former Honiton Incline signal box would have been found more at less where the rear of the train is. This was closed on 6 March 1966 and no trace of it remains today.

Above: The 1345-yard Honiton Tunnel is notable for three reasons. It is the longest tunnel on the former L&SWR, the longest in Devon and its western portal marks the summit of Honiton Bank. The structure is dead straight, with a favourable rising gradient of 1 in 132, much to the relief of the former firemen on Exeter-bound trains. Something that few will notice half-way through the tunnel is the 153 milepost, which marks the distance from Waterloo. Here we see not a Bulleid Pacific, or any other motive power associated with the route, but a welcome visitor making a grand exit from the tunnel and into the sunshine in the form of D1021 "Western Cavalier". It is forging its way west with 1B29, the diverted 12.30 Paddington–Plymouth on 14 April 1974. This was a difficult angle to reach, but well worth the effort, especially as it is no longer possible due to access problems and vegetation growth.

Above right: Two more rare visitors to the line; on 16 October 1977, 40081 & 40083 work 1Z30, the 07.30 Paddington–Par, which they hauled as far as Exeter St Davids. Both are whistling well, providing a reminder of the noise their forebears made, namely the Southern Region's Bulleid diesels of the early 1950s. They have begun descending the 1 in 80 gradient from Honiton Tunnel, which is now over a mile behind them, on the long straight approach to Honiton. This view is from the A35 road bridge. Even though this is exotic motive power for the area, believe it or not, there were some disappointed passengers on board. The train was advertised as bringing a Deltic to Devon, but due to an industrial dispute, BR's Eastern Region was unable to provide one. The photographers were not complaining though. Despite the limitations of the single line, there were sufficient gaps to allow additional trains to run between the two-hourly services, although this came at the cost of what could be a lengthy wait in one of the loops. It is still possible to take a picture from the road bridge here, but the foreground is now cluttered with lineside equipment and foliage, and the fields on the right have been replaced by a housing estate as Honiton's population grows.

Right: More railtour action at Honiton on 29 March 1975 sees D1036 "Western Emperor" on 1Z58, the 07.15 Plymouth–Derby "Western Sunset". D1036 hauled this to Westbury, where D1052 took over. The loco glistens in the morning sunshine, despite its somewhat shabby appearance, and it sounded good too, as it waited for 33046 to arrive with the 06.30 Waterloo–Exeter. The 20-minute stop allowed adequate time for photography, with the hardy like myself making it out of the station and onto the nearby road bridge. A large gallery can be seen waiting for 33046 on both the platform and the footbridge which must be undergoing something of a weight test. The footbridge was replaced by a new structure at the west end of the station in August 2009. This tour was run jointly by the Plymouth and Wirral Railway Circles and I had helped to organise it. I travelled to New York the following day to commence my secondment with Brit Rail Travel International. I was based there for the next six months and that was followed by a grand tour of North America which included the Rockies by train, so it would be mid-October before I would see another Western.

Above: Honiton station is 155 miles from Waterloo and it opened with the line in 1860. It is conveniently located for this most important of market towns in East Devon which is famed for its lace. It was, and still is, one of the busiest stations on the section between Yeovil Junction and Exeter, yet somehow this didn't seem to feature in the minds of those who planned the timetables during the eras of the Southern Railway and BR's Southern Region. Most express services ran non-stop through here, whereas they did stop at the junctions with the branch lines and locations such as Axminster, Yeovil and Sherborne. Consequently, Honiton passengers travelling to and from the east had to make use of the stopping services that began and ended at Yeovil Junction. The revised services that began with the coming of the diesel era in September 1964 did however give Honiton a much improved service to and from the east. This further improved when the Class 159s were introduced in 1993, such that Honiton now has as many daily trains to and from Waterloo than it used to have during the five-day working week. Honiton has always benefitted from local traffic to Exeter, and this was catered for to a limited extent when morning and evening commuter trains to Exeter were pathed to run between the two-hourly services to Waterloo. One such working is shown here; the 18.35 Axminster–Exeter, which is formed of Class 101 set 871. The unit had been drafted in during the rolling stock crisis which affected local services in the South West when the Class 142s were introduced (this will be mentioned when we reach Exeter Central). The unit is waiting for the 18.20 Exeter–Waterloo to arrive before it continues west on the single track line. During the privatisation era, South West Trains and its successor South Western Railway have had a monopoly on services between Salisbury and Exeter. This was only broken at the start of the December 2022 timetable, when GWR invaded the route by extending the 16.34 Barnstaple–Exeter Central to Axminster, taking a useful 17.48 commuter path out of Exeter St Davids. Strangely, this returns as empty stock, often by continuing east to Yeovil Junction, then to Yeovil Pen Mill and Castle Cary where it reverses, before returning to Exeter via Taunton. Doubtless this is to ensure route knowledge is maintained for the Exeter-based GWR crews. As Devon County Council looks to boost its Devon Metro scheme for the railways that feed Exeter, any more capacity between Honiton and Pinhoe can only come by the provision of at least one new passing loop, which it is reputed will be in the Whimple area.

Above right: This rarely-seen backlit view at Honiton can only be captured when the evening sun moves this far round during the summer. It was taken from the former Up sidings which were taken out of use on 2 May 1967, as a precursor to the singling of the route later that month. Do not be fooled by the appearance of a double track line though, as this is the passing loop. The train leaving Honiton for Exeter has been diverted this way due to the Easter Sunday diversions of 14 April 1974. D1010 "Western Campaigner" is about to take the single line to Pinhoe with 1B45, the 16.30 Paddington–Penzance. This was one of the stalwarts of the class, noted for its fine performances and overall reliability, making it very highly regarded among the enthusiast fraternity. D1010 was one of the last four Westerns to remain in service, holding out until the very end of the Hydraulic era. It was withdrawn on 28 February 1977 after its final duty of being standby engine for the now-legendary Western Tribute railtour the previous day. Note the red brick building with a flat roof on the far left. This is Honiton signal box, which opened on 16 June 1957 as one of the first replacements for the ancient L&SWR structures along the route. It would have a longer life than some of the others in the scheme which were destroyed after less than a decade in service, by virtue of Honiton being the sole crossing loop between Chard Junction and Pinhoe after the line was singled in 1967. The box would survive until the Basingstoke panel extension of March 2012 and it has since been demolished. I suspect that few railwaymen from the L&SWR or BR's Southern Region, or indeed passengers or enthusiasts, would have ever conceived that Honiton in Devon would be controlled by someone over 100 miles away in Basingstoke, which technology now allows.

Above: Three miles down the line from Honiton, at Otter View, sees 50018 "Resolution" hauling 1V09, the 10.02 Basingstoke–Exeter on 30 March 1991. It has just passed the 158 milepost (from Waterloo) and traversed the four arches of Fenny Bridges Viaduct which carries the line over the River Otter. Not far from here, the river's water supplies the Otter Brewery which produces some excellent ales. Notice how straight this section of railway is, as it descends the 1 in 100 gradient towards Exeter. Sadly, this is another location that is now obscured by vegetation growth, the shot now only being possible from a head-on angle.

Above: These next two images were taken from the same location as the previous photograph, but look in the other direction (towards Exeter). I could not resist the inclusion of a relatively modern then and now scene, where the motive power will be familiar to many because the gap between the two images is only 13 years. The peaceful fields of East Devon are a very long way from the hustle and bustle of London and its many other Network SouthEast trains. On 31 May 1990, 50003 "Temeraire" makes its way east with 1O35, the 10.20 Exeter–Waterloo.

Above right: Those quiet fields are no more, as the location is now consumed by the new alignment of the A30 which opened in 1999 , running from a junction with the M5 near Exeter. In 1996 the proposed dual carriageway made national headlines, with "Swampy's Last Stand", which referred to an eco-warrior who spent a week in a tunnel at Fairmile, not far from here, in an attempt to halt construction work. Perhaps he made a valid point, as the new road now makes it quicker for the commuters from this part of Devon to add to Exeter's chronic traffic jams. One wonders what dividends would have been paid if the money was instead used to build a new passing loop so that the line here could instead have a better passenger service. At least the new bridge is wide enough for a double track line, unlike the one to the west which carries the M5 over the railway near Pinhoe. On 15 March 2003, the only main line registered diesel hydraulic, D1015 "Western Champion" heads east with 1Z32, the 13.36 Okehampton–Crewe Western Quarryman railtour. The loco was painted in Golden Ochre livery at the time, which I think did not suit it.

Right: Having descended the two miles from Fenny Bridges, mostly at 1 in 100, the railway reaches Feniton which is 159.25 miles from Waterloo. This view looks towards Exeter from Green Lane overbridge, with the small station and its adjacent level crossing just visible beyond the train. 45111 "Grenadier Guardsman" passes with 1M91, the diverted 09.05 Plymouth–Liverpool Lime Street on 14 April 1974. The Peak would work as far as Bristol, before returning west on 1V72, a Leeds to Penzance service. Like Seaton Junction to the east, Feniton was "out in the sticks" among a few sprawling farms and houses. The station had several name changes. When it opened along with the line on 19 July 1860 it was named Feniton, before becoming Ottery Road on 1 July 1861, highlighting that it was just under three miles from the town of Ottery St Mary. It then became Ottery St Mary Sidmouth Road in April 1868, before being renamed Sidmouth Junction upon the opening of the Sidmouth branch on 6 July 1874. It retained that name until it lost its passenger services and the Sidmouth branch closed on 6 March 1967, seeing its final goods traffic two months later. The line was then singled through it on 21 May 1967, but that was not to be the end of the story. After the closure of the station, staff were retained to control the level crossing and BR had not been in any rush to demolish the platforms. Considerable housing had been built at Feniton, to the point that when the local Residents Association petitioned for the station to reopen, in an unusual development for the times, their request was granted. A reconditioned short section of the former Down platform was returned to use from 3 May 1971 and the station reverted to its original name, Feniton. Sadly the original 1860 building was replaced by a much less substantial hut. Initially the trains that stopped there were to serve the commuters, but passenger numbers kept on growing and the station was refurbished in 1993. Today Feniton station flourishes, with almost all services in each direction calling there. Of its predecessor Sidmouth Junction, there is little to recall; careful study of this 1974 picture shows little of what was there just seven years earlier.

Above: This photograph was taken from the level area that can be seen to the left of 45111 in the previous image. It was the site of two lengthy sidings that were often filled with lines of wagons carrying coal for Exmouth Junction shed. The area on the left of where the rear of both trains are is where the Sidmouth Branch began, with the line curving away to the left. In the days when my BR lineside permit allowed such ventures, this powerful low level portrait of 50039 "Implacable" was captured in superb late autumn light. It is accelerating away from Feniton after stopping there with 1O18, the 14.20 Exeter–Waterloo on 28 November 1981. Sadly both this and the view of 45111 are now obscured by a combination of vegetation growth and new housing which provides good business for the railway.

Above right: This is the Feniton of old on 2 April 1966, when it was Sidmouth Junction, with the goods shed to the left and the Up platform on the right, still with its Pullman camping coach in the bay. Behind the train is the roof of the original 1860 station building, the footbridge and above this the upper arm of the co-acting Down starting signal is visible. D7069 is waiting to depart, having backed onto the rear of the Steam Again Over Honiton Railtour, the 08.55 from Waterloo which had arrived behind 4-6-2 Pacific 34006 "Bude". The Hymek is about to take the passengers to Exmouth by way of the route via Tipton St John's (where the branch to Sidmouth deviates) and Budleigh Salterton. These routes and stations would all close in March 1967, less than a year later, and few traces of them remain. Notice the green-coloured Southern Region station nameboard on the left, which reads "Sidmouth Junction change for Ottery St Mary, Tipton St Johns, Sidmouth, Budleigh Salterton ETC". As far as I know, this was the only location where a nameboard invited passengers to change for "Et cetera", although I am happy to be corrected if any readers know different! Many station nameboards invited passengers to change for here, there and everywhere, but the ultimate condensation of where one could change for multitudinous destinations must have been Manningtree in East Anglia, where the nameboard simply proclaimed "Manningtree for Harwich branch and the Continent".

Right: Nine years later and I am back at the same location, standing on what remains of the Up platform, just a few yards forward from where the April 1966 photograph was taken. This is one of the very few Class 52 hauled trains to have ever called at the reopened Feniton station, the short platform of which is out of sight behind the coaches. D1036 "Western Emperor" had paused for a photostop, while in charge of the Western Sunset railtour on 29 March 1975. The disused part of the Down platform is visible on the left, after its edging stones have been removed. No more do the footbridge or semaphore signals reside here and instead of the camping coach and Up bay platform on the right, new housing is encroaching. The first two coaches are beside the short section of reinstated platform that comprises the recently-reopened station, allowing the camera-clad brigade to alight. Today's trains can only stop at platforms that are long enough to accommodate all the coaches, unless there is a specified local exception and selective door operation comes into play. I cannot see this sort of thing happening now, even though we all lived to tell the tale.

Above: Heading west from Feniton the line takes what is best described as a lengthy S bend that passes through the rural farms and fields that are typical of this part of East Devon. The autumn colours are beginning to appear as 50048 "Dauntless" heads round the curve that forms the first part of the S bend near Tallaton, with 1V11, the 11.15 Waterloo–Exeter on 2 November 1990. The train is seen from the overbridge on the minor road from Bittery Cross to Plymtree, near Lashbrook Farm which is to the left. The original farm buildings lay directly on the course of the line here. They therefore had to be demolished and the L&SWR rebuilt them nearer to the farm in the style of the day. Although the vegetation has increased, this angle is still available for a decent picture.

Above right: The bridge from which the previous photograph was taken can be seen in the background, on the curve beyond the train. The line here climbs on a gentle 1 in 100 gradient, with a barely noticeable summit not far short of this next bridge which carries the road from Ottery St Mary to Cullompton, not far from the village of Tallaton. 50025 "Invincible" is passing the 161 milepost (from Waterloo) on 5 April 1986. At the time, Large Logo livery locomotives and blue & grey coaches were the normal daily diet here, but a closer look reveals that the train is formed of Mark 2 air-conditioned stock, with a Mark 1 buffet coach. That's because this is 1C48, the 13.25 Paddington–Penzance, which was diverted via Yeovil that day due to engineering work on the GWR main line. Waterloo to Exeter passengers were never graced with air-conditioned stock. Talaton was not considered important enough to be granted its own station, instead the road to Feniton was thought to be adequate for local transport needs. Sadly, the loco proved to be anything but Invincible. It was derailed at West Ealing, while running at high speed on an Oxford to Paddington service on 6 August 1989, after vandals placed a length of rail on the track. The engine was damaged beyond economic repair and was scrapped at Old Oak Common depot two months later. Due to substantial growth here, only a head-on view of passing trains is now obtainable and the bridge by Lashbrook Farm is totally obscured.

Above: Here the East Devon countryside looks its best on a fine spring evening. According to the Network Rail plaque, this location is Lil Davys Bridge on the Whimple road, which is a mile on from the bridge in the previous image. Sunny View Farm is to the right. The line here descends towards Whimple on a 1 in 100 gradient. D1003 "Western Pioneer" heads west with 1B33, the diverted 14.30 Paddington–Penzance on 14 April 1974. On the left are Talaton Cottages, which were built by the L&SWR for its employees. During the 1950s they were the homes of a couple of permanent way staff and their families. Until 1958, residents of the cottages had no running water, receiving it instead by a novel method; the 13.35 Exmouth Junction–Honiton local goods train would stop here on Mondays, Wednesdays and Fridays to deliver cans of water and pick up the empties. Now that the cottages have been refurbished and modernised, they make desirable residences, with conditions that the former gangers and their kin probably never imagined. A recent visit here found the railway running through a dense tree lined avenue and that the cottages would have no view of passing trains.

Above: About 20 minutes after D1003 had made its way west, D1056 "Western Sultan" came purring along in the other direction with 1A75, the diverted 14.00 Penzance–Paddington. It is on the straight section from Whimple, which is 1.75 miles distant. The Western made a memorable sound ascending the 1 in 100 gradient, disturbing the peace and quiet of the spring evening with music to the ears! On this side of the bridge the foliage has grown but not to the same extent; standing a tad to the left a reasonable picture can still be taken.

Above right: This pleasant scene is typical of the period. 33119 ambles through the loop at Whimple with 1V15, the 15.00 Waterloo–Exeter on 9 April 1977. The station opened with the line on 19 July 1860, at a point 163.75 miles from Waterloo and is situated conveniently for the nearby village. It escaped the local station cull of March 1966, as it was used by a good complement of commuters, mostly to and from Exeter. When the route was singled, the Down main line was retained and the Up line through the station (on the left) became a loop siding that was controlled from two new ground frames at either end of it. These gave access to the goods yard, which closed to public traffic on 4 December 1967, and to the private siding that served Whiteways Cider. This company's premises were adjacent to the goods yard until cider production ceased in 1989. Cider (and the stronger scrumpy) does however, continue to be made from the produce of the area's orchards. During October and November 1992, to accommodate the forthcoming Class 159s, which were longer than the existing DMUs, the loop was removed and the Up platform was extended out over the area that the loop occupied. The work left a single platform, which may have been more convenient for local passengers who no longer had to cross the footbridge to access trains (the bridge was relocated to Grateley), but it did nothing to aid the capacity constraints on the single line section. Had the loop been retained, then it could have been returned to main line use to provide some much-needed additional capacity on the section between Honiton and Pinhoe. Whimple does at least now have the most frequent train service it has ever seen. On the left, parked outside the station, is my little Ford Prefect 100E which bore replica "Western Empire" nameplates. These had been recently applied after a slide show that involved much real ale drinking in tribute to the recent passing of the Class 52s – no prizes for guessing which one was my favourite!

Right: Pinhoe station is 168.5 miles from Waterloo and did not open with the line in 1860. The hamlet grew into a small village and became important enough to be granted a station on 30 October 1871, before it was closed nearly 95 years later on 7 March 1966. As time subsequently passed, Pinhoe went from being a village in the country to a suburb of Exeter. Consequently, to serve the demand for local journeys, the station reopened on 6 May 1983, enabling commuters and shoppers alike to reach the centre of Exeter in a matter of minutes. The station now enjoys an excellent and well-used train service in both directions. This picture was taken on 27 April 1982, with the platforms looking bare and untidy because it would be more than a year before they regained a passenger service. Southern Region celebrity engines 73142 "Broadlands" and 33027 "Earl Mountbatten of Burma" await their passage onto the single line section towards Honiton. The pair were returning home to Eastleigh after being exhibits at the recently-held Laira Depot open day. "Broadlands" was a very rare visitor to these parts as the Class 73s hardly ever ventured anywhere on the West of England main line beyond Worting Junction, which they would pass through on the electrified route to the south coast. The road bridge beyond 33027 is our next port of call.

Above: This period piece from the A38 road bridge (now the B3181) at Pinhoe shows D810 "Cockade" hauling 1O12, the 12.28 Exeter–Waterloo on 14 September 1971. Pinhoe station is behind the camera, on the other side of the bridge. The single line section begins to the east of Pinhoe station, under the control of Exmouth Junction signal box; the interface with the Basingstoke Panel is on the single line at milepost 167 and the electronics are controlled by track circuit block working. Note the wartime sidings on the right; these were installed in 1943 to serve a Ministry of Food frozen food store, which is the large brick and concrete building in the background. This was built to a standard wartime design, with extra storage space being provided by the Nissen Huts adjacent to the main line. In 1971 these were being used by the firm Marley Tiles. The rusting sidings had been taken out of use two years earlier in 1969 and would be removed in 1979.

Above right: 18 years later and we have another period piece at the same location with a different type of Warship. 50049 "Defiance" passes with the same train, the 12.28 Exeter–Waterloo, which now has the headcode 1O37, on 24 June 1989. The telegraph poles have gone and the rather battered gate is the only reminder of the former wartime sidings. The Nissen huts look like they are about to fall down, while the former frozen food store does at least appear to still be in good repair. Those buildings were all swept away in 2009 though, to make way for new housing and tree growth much impedes the view today. A piece of Pinhoe that survives, albeit about 60 miles away, is its signal box. This closed on 13 February 1988, when a new mini panel in Exmouth Junction signal box took over. The box was then relocated to the Tamar Belle Heritage Centre at Bere Ferrers station.

Right: 88 miles on from Salisbury, the journey from Waterloo to the West Country reaches a significant railway centre, the city of Exeter. This view from Howell Road overbridge sees 50020 "Revenge" passing some fine examples of Southern Region signalling with 1V11, the 11.10 Waterloo–Exeter on 26 April 1982. In the foreground is the Exeter Central A signal box home signal, a fine three-arm bracket, the middle arm of which is raised for the train to enter the station's Down platform. The lower arm on the right is for the Down bay platform and that to the left is for the station's through centre road. The rusting rails on the right are the two carriage sidings, and the Up Main line and Up loop are visible on the left.

Above: This locomotive is a rare visitor to the West of England main line and indeed to anywhere this far west. The unique 47901 approaches Exeter Central with 1Z37, the 07.27 Birmingham New Street–Meldon Quarry "Meldon Quarryman" railtour, which it worked between Westbury and Exeter St Davids on 7 June 1987. Notice how much the view looking east from the bridge has altered in the five years since the previous picture was taken. The changes were in the main brought about by the Exeter Panel signal box taking over the area in May 1985. The building to the right of the train is a relay room for the panel. Above it more modern architecture now marks the scene and the line on the far left has been lifted. The former D1628, 47046 (from November 1973) and 47601 (from December 1975) became 47901 in November 1979, forming its own sub class with just one representative. To cut a long and technical story very short, as 47901 the locomotive became the test bed for what would become the Class 58 engine and it was scrapped at MC Metals Glasgow in February 1992.

Above right: From the same place and on the same day as the above photograph of 50020 was taken arriving from Waterloo, this was the view looking in the other direction five minutes later. The rear of 50020's train is just visible as 50017 "Royal Oak" brings 1O18, the 14.20 Exeter–Waterloo out of Exeter Central. On the right is Exeter Central A signal box, which in 1982 was the only box controlling the station, as B box at its west end had closed on 23 February 1970 when the layout was simplified and A box lost its suffix. The former A box would close on 6 May 1985, when the Exeter Panel (located at St Davids) took over control of the area, as far as a fringe at Exmouth Junction. As with the view in the opposite direction, significantly less railway infrastructure is now visible from the overbridge, compared to what could be seen four decades ago. The carriage sidings on the left, and signal box and cattle pens on the right have all disappeared. Just two lines now pass beneath the road bridge that 50017 is approaching. The siding to the bay platform on the far left is the only other line that remains, although this now only sees intermittent use, such as during times of service disruption.

Right: The line from Salisbury to Exeter opened on 19 July 1860, with Exeter's new Queen Street terminus providing convenient access to the city centre. It became the changing point for the Exmouth branch when this opened on 1 May 1861, beginning from a junction just over a mile to the east. Queen Street became a through station the following year, when the steeply graded 1 in 37 semi-circular link down to Exeter St Davids opened on 1 February 1862. Since then it has seen many changes and the station we recognise today is the result of various improvements that were completed between 1925 and 1933; the track layout was improved and the original timber Down and Up line trainsheds were replaced, as both were disliked by passengers and staff alike, due to their cramped layout and the air seemingly always being full of engine smoke. The SR then constructed a new station facade and brick buildings which can still be admired today. The platforms were also rebuilt, opening on 1 July 1933. These could accommodate 14-coach trains and bay platforms were added at the Salisbury end, adjacent to both the Up and Down through platforms. At the same time in 1933, the station was renamed Exeter Central. This photograph was taken on 13 September 1980, by which time it had become rather run down. The Up through line had been taken out of use on 9 November 1969. Public goods traffic had ceased in the yard on the right from 4 December 1967, but it continued to handle Blue Circle Cement traffic from Westbury until January 1990. The sound of a Warship or Western dragging a cement train up the bank from Exeter St Davids was something to be savoured. The site of the yard is now covered by housing. The Down through line lasted until 13 October 1984 and this has also been removed, leaving a large open space. 33027 "Earl Mountbatten

of Burma" has arrived with 1O24, the 18.20 Exeter–Waterloo. This is one of two celebrity Class 33s that didn't survive into preservation. Traction on the line to Waterloo was in the process of being transferred to Class 50s at the time and shortly after 33027 left, 50024 arrived with the 15.10 from Waterloo. With nine coaches in tow, Type 3 traction wasn't ideal for the route, as the locos had to accelerate and brake hard repeatedly on its high-speed sections. These regular bursts of speed were not ideal for the Class 50s either, as the Type 4s were built for long-distance non-stop running and their early days on the route were marked by unreliability problems. They did however improve the timings slightly.

Above: During the early diesel era, on 20 June 1970, the two children do not seem to be interested in D804 "Avenger", which is waiting to proceed with 1O18, the 18.05 Exeter–Waterloo, or the unidentified Class 22 that is lurking in the sidings beyond the station. Exeter Central had changed little in appearance during the preceding decades, although the SR would not have allowed weeds to appear on the platform. Most of the infrastructure dated back to the SR, including the signals, the lamps, the station nameboard and the fine footbridge which showcases the produce of Exmouth Junction Concrete Works. Standing here today gives a very different view, with modern lampposts, new signage and a 21st century footbridge that provides wheelchair access. The recently-installed bridge also allowed the reopening of what was known as the Passimeter, a pedestrian entrance giving direct access to Queen Street (the Western Region had closed this to reduce staff costs). The station's 1933 layout facilitated the joining of the various portions that arrived from North Devon and North Cornwall and the adding or detaching of the restaurant cars on expresses to and from Waterloo. These movements were carried out with speed and efficiency, which is perhaps something that the present-day operator GWR could learn from with regards to joining and splitting their five-coach Class 800s! Such things came to an end with the timetable changes of 7 September 1964, which was the dawn of the diesels on main line services, although some local trains and those on the Exmouth Branch had been DMU-operated since 1963. Eastbound local services had been withdrawn in March 1966, meaning that at the time of this picture, Exeter Central was only served by infrequent trains towards Salisbury and those to Exmouth. It was when the signalling was brought under the control of the Exeter Panel in 1985 that BR's Western Region recognised Exeter Central's potential. For example, the heavily-used Paignton to Exeter St Davids local services were amalgamated with those on the Exmouth branch. This was made possible by the Down line from Exeter Central to St Davids being bi-directionally signalled, meaning the DMU driver could simply change ends and reverse, saving passengers from having to change trains (or walk or catch a bus between the two stations). This led to a healthy increase in passenger numbers. The Network SouthEast era then brought a dash of colour to Exeter Central, until BR transferred responsibility for the station to the Regional Railways sector.

Below: This photograph was taken on 20 June 1970, six years on from when Exeter Central was bustling with so much more activity. By 1970 things had reached a low ebb, with only around eight daily trains to or from the Salisbury direction, plus Exmouth services and the odd working from North Devon that crept its way up the bank from St Davids. In a scene that had changed little since the golden era, three-car Class 118 set P467 stands in an unusual location, on the Down through line. The DMU had been parked there to make way for a special train that is out of sight behind the photographer. Class 33s D6505 and D6509 are ready to depart in top and tail formation, with a Strong & Co. Brewery staff charter from Romsey to Exmouth. The special train was taking the path of the 18.15 Exeter Central–Exmouth and the 18.45 return working, with one coach of this being designated for local branch line passengers. It is difficult to image that degree of pragmatism and flexibility being implemented on today's railway. There would also be the question of where to stable the designated unit for an hour, as virtually all through lines and sidings have been removed from today's stations. A closer examination of this image reveals that such changes are on the horizon for Exeter Central, as the rails of the Up through line are rusting away because they had been taken out of use on 9 November 1969.

Above: We now see an example of the second generation DMUs that replaced their first generation counterparts. The latter were popular with passengers due to the (mostly) comfortable ride they offered and many will remember the view of the line ahead when seated behind the driver's cab. In these respects, second generation units left a lot to be desired, especially in the case of the Class 142 Pacers, or "Skippers" as they were initially known in the West Country. As this photograph from 29 August 1987 shows, those that operated in the region from 1985 were painted in chocolate and cream livery. The concept of a Leyland National bus design on a fixed four-wheel chassis probably looked good on paper, but insufficient consideration was given to the gradients and curves on the branch lines of Devon and Cornwall. I remember being on a Class 142 to Axminster one evening and it was quite an experience, bouncing along the main line at faster than a mile a minute. When this view of 142019 was captured leaving Exeter Central with the 12.40 Exeter St Davids–Exmouth, the writing was on the wall for the units and their banishment to the North West was imminent. Two decades later, to cover for stock shortages while the Class 150 & 158s were being refurbished, a dozen Class 142s were loaned from Northern Rail in December 2007, a decision that was not a popular with the travelling public. Five of the units were returned within a year, but the rest soldiered on until a Class 142 farewell special ran on 27 November 2011, which included a run to Okehampton amongst other destinations. That wasn't the end for Pacers in Devon though, as the similar Class 143s remained in service until the end of 2020. From the start of the May 1986 summer timetable, Exmouth branch services became half-hourly during the day and the former Western and Southern Region prejudices had been overcome such that some Exmouth services continued to Paignton. Bringing the story of Exeter Central up to date sees a very different situation to that of the 1970s. The station is now served by hourly services in each direction to Waterloo, hourly trains to and from Barnstaple, half-hourly trains between Exmouth and Paignton and from May 2022 the new hourly Okehampton services began. With such an intensive schedule from so many different locations, and being so convenient for the city centre, Exeter Central is now the second busiest station in Devon. From a railway enthusiast's point of view, the traction is very boring, with a diet of Sprinters broken only by a handful of Class 166 Turbo DMUs. Like at many other stations, a locomotive hauled train is now a rare sight at Exeter Central, although what we see and photograph today will of course soon be tomorrow's history!

Reaching Exeter Central is not the end of our journey from London Waterloo to the Atlantic Coast. The second book in this two-part series continues the journey to the northern coast of both Devon and Cornwall, with a large section being devoted to the line north to Barnstaple and Ilfracombe. This second part, which will be published in mid-2024, features plenty more diesel-hydraulic and diesel-electric locomotives, plus a number diesel multiple units to add to the variety. All of the images are colour, which is rare for many of the locations included, such as Torrington, Barnstaple, Ilfracombe, Lydford, Tavistock, Halwill, Wadebridge, Padstow and Bude.